Jesus
& Company

Part I

by
Don and Sondra Tipton

Via Verde Publishing

Jesus & Company
Editor - Dorothy Miller
Editing by Chuck Dean
Copy Editing by Donna Goodrich
Typesetting by Jan Carroll
Cover Design - Tim Ramos

ISBN 0-9645307-0-8

Published by:
Via Verde Publishing
43500 Cactus Valley Road
Hemet, CA 92544

Printed in the United States.
10 9 8 7 6 5 4 3 2

TABLE OF CONTENTS

Vinicio Alvarez

Doug Ford pictured here
with his family

DEDICATION

This book is dedicated to the precious memory of Doug
Ford and Vinicio Alvarez, two men who gave their lives in service
to the Lord.

"Spirit" Ship Chaplain Doug Ford and "Spirit" Ship Chief
Steward Vinicio Alvarez died of cerebral malaria contracted deep
in Africa during a ship's mission. Doug Ford died on Good Friday
and was buried at sea on Easter Sunday. He is survived by his loving
family, his wife Carla, son Justin and daughter Melissa. Vinicio
died on the Atlantic coast of South America two weeks later.

Jesus said, *"Greater love has no one than this, that he lay
down his life for his friends."* In their young lives, these two loving
men laid down their lives for their friends, for their neighbors, and
for those they did not even know and were never to meet, as they
touched thousands, spreading the good news of the Gospel and
providing physical help to people in nations throughout the world.

The work of "Friend Ships" will forever include the
memory of these two men and the foundation they laid for the work
of the ministry as they gave their all for the cause of Christ.

PREFACE

We come not as ministers, theologians or experts of any kind. We come as witnesses, testifying to the reality of God's "book of words" and to the love and faithfulness of Jesus Christ, our Lord.

This book is about ordinary people in unusual circumstances with an extraordinary God. It is a record of miracles that occur daily, not miracles to merely get us started or occasionally scattered here and there, but miracles occurring each day—keeping mighty ships at sea, and providing food to hungry masses around the world.

PUBLISHER PREFACE

The Holy Bible begins and ends with displays of God's supernatural power. Scripture pages resound with records of God's mighty works, both in the earth and in the lives of His people. Most Christians read, and thoroughly believe, in the biblical miracles. They also know that Jesus Christ is *"the same yesterday, today and forever,"* yet few expect to see God's supernatural intervention today in their own lives. Most say, "God can do the impossible," yet never personally choose the risk of taking the Lord at His Word.

When God created people, He asked for their trust, but since that time, only a few—a very few— have stepped out in faith and put the Lord's promises to the test. God has never failed them.

George Mueller of the nineteenth became known as that person of faith. Now, one hundred years later, this book, Jesus & Company recounts the story of two more such people. This volunteer couple, the Tiptons, dare daily to walk in faith and believe in God's miraculous ability and desire to provide for His children.

Because of space, they record in this book only a small fraction of the wonderful stories, miraculous answers to prayer and names of the committed volunteers who have joined them in this "faith ministry." As God provides time and resources, we hope to publish more volumes to the praise and honor of our wonderful Lord.

Readers cannot dismiss this book as "a wonderful account of a holy man and woman." No, indeed! This is the record of many ordinary Christians—from all walks of life—who are daring to set aside temporal goals and comforts in order to serve their living and powerful Lord.

When reading these pages, it is not enough just to marvel over God's strength and tender concern. We must each ask ourselves, **"Have I** gone far enough yet with God?"

FOREWORD

Don Tipton is without a doubt one of the most amazing men I have ever met. His grasp of the awesomeness of God is unbelievable.

If any man has removed the word "can't" from his every action and thought, it is Don Tipton. Godly, selfless, helpful, caring and intelligent, along with the greatest faith I have ever seen, describes this marvelous man.

This book will lift you to plateaus of faith and trust you have not yet comprehended. It is a must read for anyone willing to do the impossible for God.

Tommy Barnett

1

INTO SOVIET WATERS

A day and a half outside of Soviet waters, gunboats appeared on the horizon, observing us, then dropping back to starboard. It was August 1991, the atmosphere tense and eerie. The gunboats remained several hundred yards away while a patrol boat appeared on our stern. We studied the occupants with our binoculars, discovering that they also had their binoculars turned on us. Suddenly, another military ship appeared off our bow. To our surprise, a large cruiser loomed dead ahead, then nosed out of sight. Throughout the afternoon it kept disappearing, then reappearing.

As the day wore on, military ships surrounded us—one to port, one to starboard, one astern and the cruiser across our bow. One of our crew members joked, "We haven't heard the news in weeks. There could have been a military coup here and we wouldn't even know it had happened!"

Our ship's agent in Germany had promised to telex our estimated time of arrival to the U.S.S.R. maritime authority, but we had no confirmation that contact had actually been made.

Proper maritime protocol is to display the flag of the country in whose waters you are sailing, so as we entered Soviet waters and approached the port of Riga, we raised the red flag of the U.S.S.R. with its yellow hammer and sickle. Because these waters had been Latvian before that nation was taken over by communism, we raised the burgundy and white striped Latvian flag beneath the hammer and sickle. Our American stars and

11

stripes continued to wave proudly from the stern.

Our written sailing directions told us which radio channel to use in order to communicate with the Soviets. We tried repeatedly but got no response.

Finally, an operator came back and commanded us to switch to a new channel. Excitedly we complied.

A voice in English, but heavy with Slavic accent, crackled through the airwaves: "Identify yourself!" Our chief mate responded, "Motor vessel Spirit." The Slavic voice asked him to repeat it. The mate then spelled out the vessel's name in maritime phonetics: "Motor vessel Spirit—Sierra, Papa, India, Romeo, India, Tango." There was a long silence and then came the request again. "Motor vessel Spirit, repeat, Spirit. How many people? How much cargo?" the voice demanded. We responded, "We are the mercy vessel Spirit, an American flagship carrying food, clothing and medicine to bless your people in need." The radio fell silent.

On Sunday, August 18, we made our final approach into Riga. We were the first American ship to sail into this Baltic harbor for sixteen years! Riga's port was known as a stronghold of military strength that housed a large reserve of navy vessels. We sailed quietly past a nuclear submarine base as "our" gunboat escorts continued to tail us. Finally, a Soviet tug came alongside the ship and ushered us into port.

We berthed the Spirit and tied off our lines. Glaring at us as we lowered the plank that spanned from the ship to the gangway, KGB guards took position at the base of the gangway. Others took stations at our bow and stern. Some stood watch in dock-side towers that loomed above the ship. When I focused our video camera in the direction of the gangway guards, they shook their heads and made fists at me.

One remaining gunboat which had followed us into the harbor dropped anchor a few hundred yards away. We could still see military personnel on deck observing us with binoculars. As night fell, they bathed us with powerful searchlights, scanning the ship from one end to the other, a routine they continued throughout every night.

In the morning, we had a prayer meeting followed by breakfast, and then prepared for our first day of cargo operations in the ominous Soviet Union. Because all arrangements for the mission had been made with the Gorbachev government well in advance of our arrival, we were confident our unloading would transpire smoothly. We had received all necessary permission to discharge 4,000 tons of humanitarian aid for church distribution throughout the U.S.S.R. The Soviets had also guaranteed us that all fees would be waived.

However, at nine a.m. Boris Iofis, a lawyer who had been completing all our paperwork, arrived at the ship bearing grim news. Solemnly, he took me aside to tell me quietly that Mikhail Gorbachev, President of the Soviet Union, had been kidnapped or perhaps even killed. All international broadcasts and free television had been blacked out.

The streets of Riga soon filled with Soviet tanks and armored personnel carriers. Riga's port was sealed, the road to Leningrad barricaded, and all telecommunications cut off. Now, martial law ruled. Members of the elite killer forces, the dreaded "Black Beret," patrolled the streets, suppressing any possible Latvian rebellion. Laws of the Baltic states and all other republics were nullified and their Parliaments were disbanded—only Soviet law was in effect.

Yes, as hard as it was to believe, the Soviet Union was in the midst of a full-blown, hard line communist coup d'état! Stunned, I excused myself from Boris and walked up to the ship's bridge to try and sort out what to do. The world reeled because of what had just happened and so did I.

Seventy-five men, women and children, a multimillion dollar vessel and eight million dollars worth of cargo under my leadership were suddenly, and unexpectedly, tied up in a very hostile port. I had led these faithful and innocent volunteers to rebuild this old ship, load it up with supplies and sail thousands of miles across two oceans to deliver the love of Jesus in the form of Bibles, food, clothing and medical supplies to our Soviet brothers and sisters who were hungry and in need. *What have I done?* I thought. *I've brought unsuspecting people, who simply trusted in God's mission, straight into the arms of a hard-line communist takeover in the feared and ruthless U.S.S.R.!*

Standing there on the bridge, I began to remember the comfortable life my wife and I had lived just a few short years ago as owners of the Beverly Hills area Park West Polo and Hunt Club. I then thought, *Lord, how on earth did we get here?* My life up to this point began to play back through my mind as I stood looking out at this hostile harbor, so far away from California.

2

A CHANGE IN DIRECTION

Growing up in Newhall, California, mother made sure that we regularly attended church. Then, at thirteen I invited Jesus Christ into my heart. It was a profound experience—one I'd never forget. Therefore throughout the years, I always considered myself a Christian. God faithfully watched over me, bringing His men in and out of my life. But my way of living was a lukewarm, quasi-Christian existence, with a base of Jello, nothing firm, in my commitment. The word "unreal" would best apply. Twenty-six years later, my major focus was operating a hunter-jumper horse ranch in Brentwood, California, and the ownership of an exclusive equestrian polo club in Pacific Palisades. By then any real interest in Christ had mostly faded away. Jesus was no longer a part of my conscious life.

One summer day, a young woman named Sondra paid a visit to the polo club. That was the first time we met and we were drawn to each other right away. As our friendship developed, I saw that Sondra was searching desperately for a relationship with God. She felt like a rat in a trap, telling me she had determined that "freedom isn't in therapy, social action, meditation or physics, and it sure isn't in the stars."

Even though I wasn't following Jesus myself, whenever I saw Sondra cry out for peace and meaning in her life, I couldn't help but tell her what I knew. I told her how the Son of God had died to pay for her sins—how she could invite Him to come into her life.

The Polo Club, a time long past

As I talked, she listened, sometimes bored, sometimes angry, sometimes polite, but never really interested. During one of these seemingly fruitless conversations, I said, "Talking to God is like sending out radio air waves and the only channel that reaches the Father is the Son. If you really want to contact God, speak to Him through His Son, Jesus."

For some reason, that simple illustration stuck in her mind. Weeks later she asked me to tell her again how to tune in to that airwave called Jesus. I told her reluctantly, knowing our lives together would never again be the same. Just how crucial this change was going to be, I could never have imagined.

That night Sondra gave her heart to Jesus and soon the great change evidenced in her life drew me back into His loving arms. A few months later we were baptized, and soon after that we became husband and wife.

Business responsibilities took up our weekends, so we didn't have much opportunity to attend a regular church or to be involved with Christian friends. But we did study the Bible on our own with great intensity and with an insatiable thirst. As we searched the Scriptures, we hungered to become more involved with the Holy Spirit. Soon, we began to understand a little of the heart of God.

We read the pages that told how much He loved us, how much He loved our brothers and sisters, and how He wanted His children to help the widows, orphans and the poor. We realized that when He looked down upon the earth, He didn't see boundaries, borders, or city and county lines. He only saw His people—people that He loved.

We read the Scriptures and simply believed. No one was there to explain the Scriptures away, to tell us that verses didn't mean what they said or that they meant something else. With simplicity, we read and believed.

Before our commitment to really know the Lord, we had been caught up in our own world of lavish parties, champagne and social guests; it was our business. But now, we watched news broadcasts with new hearts. For the first time we **really saw** coverage of the horrifying famines in Ethiopia.

We saw African children starving and dying by the hundreds. Our hearts broke at the scenes of mothers leaving their children's lifeless bodies by the roadside—mothers too exhausted to carry them home for burial.

We lived in a land of plenty. While these Africans and other children of the world starved, the granaries here at home were so packed that great piles of wheat were being dumped beside highways. Unbelievably, billions of pounds of potatoes and corn were being plowed under in the fields each year to keep our market prices high.

We had a simple thought—not really understanding at the time that the Holy Spirit sometimes puts thoughts into our minds. *What if we take from this land of plenty what it doesn't want, what it is spending millions of dollars each year to burn and bury? What if we take the crumbs from the tables of the wealthy and share them with our brothers and sisters and children who are poor and starving? If there truly is a need —and there is—if we are our brother's keeper and it is our job to help the poor, the widows, the orphans and those in need, if the Lord is the great provider, and if we were willing and said, "Here we are, Lord, send us," would He really supply? If someone was willing to love these children in need, if someone did it for the glory of God, would the Lord turn His face from them?*

A few months before we turned our lives over to Jesus, Sondra and I had been working with the Gaming Alliance of Nevada. This group consisted of the heads of some of the biggest casinos, such as Caesar's Palace and Harrah's.

The Alliance flew us to Nevada four days a week, where we were picked up by limousine or given a new Lincoln to drive. We lived at the casinos, and in addition to the healthy salaries we earned, our rooms, meals and any alcohol we cared to consume were provided free of charge for us and our invited guests. Our job was to target the lightest casino attendance days of the year and plan special attractions that would draw people into town and to the gaming tables.

We produced rock concerts, country-western shows, truck pulls and other events. We would invite polo players and celebrity friends to the activities. The Alliance would fly these stars in, provide free hotel rooms, drinks and meals just so they would greet visitors and sign autographs. Meanwhile, the casinos cashed in on extra people flocking into town for the concerts, games and events. Then each weekend we'd take a return flight to the polo club to oversee ranch operations.

During this period, various incidents that had previously seemed almost normal, now began to greatly trouble us. One example: a married couple—an extremely famous actor and actress who were friends of ours from California—flew to New York to perform in a play on Broadway. A few weeks later they missed seeing their dogs and wanted to have the pets sent to them, but couldn't bear the thought of the animals traveling in a commercial passenger plane. One dog was a very large, inbred, paranoid-schizophrenic female. The other was a huge but not quite so difficult male. Because I had a way with animals and was one of the few people these dogs liked, our friends asked me to pick them up by limousine, drive them to the Van Nuys airport and accompany them as they flew on a private, chartered Lear jet to New York.

Another time, we entertained the secret police of Mexico at the polo club. They were so drunk the day they arrived, they could barely stand on their feet, much less ride horses or play polo. Later that day, during dinner, we listened to the men make cruel jokes about poor Mexican peasants, describing how they forced them to their hands and knees in order to use the men's backs as steps to mount their horses.

Then there was the time we were invited by a sultan to play his team. He planned to fly our team of polo horses, at his expense, by 747 jet to his homeland for the match! This extravagance seemed particularly wrong when we realized that many people in his country suffered great starvation, and massive poverty was common among the general population.

Part of my business was to sell horses for the pleasure of girls and boys who rode in competition. There seemed to be no limit to the amount of money this crowd would spend on themselves or their children for their sporting pleasure. It was nothing for parents to pay $50,000 per horse so that their children could hang a ribbon on the wall.

I was part of all this insanity, even orchestrating much of it! Sondra and I watched time and time again as our friends would lavishly crack open a bottle of champagne which sold for hundreds of dollars, consume hardly a glass and then abandon the bottle. All this took place while Ethiopian mothers laid their dead children at the side of the road.

When we invited Jesus into our hearts to be Lord of our lives and as He became a real part of our existence, the contrast we saw between the "needs" of the rich and the "needs" of the poor became increasingly distressful. A stirring feeling deep inside us grew each day.

We continued to study the Scriptures; it was a time of great soul searching. Questions abounded: *Is one Scripture as true as the rest? Can we stake our eternity on some verses and ignore thousands of others? Is the Bible written for today? Is Jesus the same today as He was yesterday and as He will be tomorrow? Can we trust what the Book says? Is it really reliable, something we can live by and bank on?*

Some people tried to tell us that the Bible only contains wise words on which to reflect, general principles on which to raise our children, and nice standards on which to base our court systems.

We kept wondering, *Are these words something more? Do the Scriptures apply to us now as well as eternally? Is this Book truly holy, not because a man says it is but because it is actually the **words of God**? Can we as mortal people in this modern day and age, with all of our vast knowledge and great technological*

*progress, turn our trust from what the world offers and live a
different kind of life, with a different kind of trust? Can we simply
believe the words of the Bible and base all that we are, all that
we work for, our financial stability and the understanding of all
we've been taught, on a spiritual Book written thousands of years
ago by mystical men we know only by name? Can we rely on the
God described in that Book? Can we believe Him for **even more
than a single great event** like someone rising from a wheelchair
to the thunder of applause? If this Book is real, can we believe
Him for the needs of everyday existence and miraculous
provisions for the work He has prepared for us to do?*

We longed to work for the Lord full-time, with Him meeting
all our needs. We knew we had no credentials and wondered if
we qualified to work for Him. I had attended school until the
eighth grade but had only the equivalent of a third grade education,
only barely able to read and write, and Sondra had only just
recently found Jesus.

Although our life was comfortable, we were far from being
wealthy. We wondered what God's requirements were for going
into full-time ministry. *Did we have to go to Bible school? Did
we need a degree? Was it necessary to be rich or good looking
or smart?* We began to search the pages of the Bible to see if we
would be exempt or disqualified. *Could He use us? Would He
really take care of us?*

We discovered that the Scriptures told us not to worry about
our lives, what we would wear, what we would eat or even about
tomorrow.

Excitedly, we read that our Father knows what we need. The
pages revealed many things—like how the lilies of the field don't
labor or spin, yet not even Solomon was clothed like them. The
ravens don't sow or reap, don't have a storeroom or barn, yet
God feeds them; and we are more valuable to Him than the birds.
We were to seek His kingdom first and the things we needed
would be given to us. The Book told us to sell our possessions
and give to the poor, that God would provide purses that would

not wear out, and a treasure in heaven that wouldn't be destroyed. We read that those who help the poor are lending to the Lord, and He pays great dividends, even when the help is something as small as giving a cup of cold water. We understood that if we fed or clothed the needy or visited the sick or prisoners, it would be like doing that directly for our Lord.

Our search in the Scriptures continued and we saw that there is a plan laid out, a plan which includes people like us. The plan wasn't reserved just for priests, rabbis or preachers. In fact, the Word told us that all Christians are responsible to care for their neighbors and the poor—we **are** our brother's keeper—whoever is kind to the needy honors God—our faith is made complete by what we do.

We never saw the page where it said it was mandatory for us to go to Bible school, or be rich or even be smart. We looked, but it wasn't in there.

All of this information really prompted serious inner examination. I was turning forty. For all those years, my thoughts were only of what I wanted and how to obtain it, as my goals were to fulfill my own needs and desires. I had no concern for the man on the street and no thought for where he would sleep. I made my own destiny (I thought), and he should make his. But in all my arrogance, I couldn't find a way to live with the fact that children were hungry and in pain every night. I couldn't find a way to accept the fact that they were dying at more than 35,000 every day, that millions lived in filth, victimized by indifferent adults.

Up to this point it became apparent that I was as guilty as the other indifferent adults. If I died suddenly at forty from a heart attack caused by rich foods or perhaps from some dumb accident and came before Jesus, what would I say to Him? How would He measure my life? Beside what measuring stick would I stand? I had lived a life of self-indulgence, sometimes doing nice things and being basically a kind man, but I sure wouldn't have wanted to step on one side of the scale and be weighed against the children of poverty, hunger and pain or the man on the street. Had I died at forty, I'm afraid the scale of obedience would have read "tilt."

I knew the Bible taught that you're saved by grace, through faith, and this not from yourselves, it is the gift of God, not by works, so that no man can boast. If I died on that day (or this), I am confident of spending eternity with the Lord Jesus. But that passage in Ephesians 2 continued on to say: *"For we are God's workmanship, created in Christ Jesus to do good works, which God prepared in advance for us to do."* This Scripture was of special interest to me, because I had often heard the first section quoted from my Christian brothers, but wondered why I seldom heard reference to the second.

We weren't looking for a club to join. We owned one. We had plenty of good friends and thought our family was great. But if there was a bigger reason for being here, if we weren't just passing through this planet by chance, we wanted—we needed—to know what that reason was.

We decided to ask God. *If the Bible is true, not fairy tales, not fortune cookies or the meditation of mortal men—God, if you really love us and know how many hairs are on our heads—if you care about us more than the birds that you feed or the flowers that you clothe—if we went out and started serving you—would you stand by us? Would you be there? Could we turn loose and say, "God, catch us."*

We were determined to find out.

Sondra and I made a decision to spend the rest of our lives together in service to God. The Word of God says that for what we do on earth we will be rewarded in heaven. Believing in His Word fully, we wanted to begin to load our side of the scale.

But it was more than that. We started to realize that our lives could take a new direction, that we wouldn't be giving up anything at all. Rather we would be gaining a great promotion. We were applying to work for I AM THAT I AM, the Son of the Living God! We could actually serve under the great God of the universe—that in doing so we could live a life of meaning and real purpose—that we could express our gratitude to Him for His goodness and His love in our doing!

We were the fortunate ones, born in the land of milk and honey (with granaries running over) and free to worship God. But now we also knew we were obligated to others. The Word of God tells us over and over that "we" are responsible. Who is the Word of God talking about? Who are "we"? As Sondra and I read, we realized that "we" must mean: "we" who read and "we" who believe.

We began to realize that knowledge of the Word without putting it to the test is only knowledge, that it's easy to say we believe and trust God; the hard part would be **putting our faith to work.**

Through the years, I've discovered that making the decision to follow Christ is not so hard. The real test comes when we decide what restrictions we will place on that commitment—"This far and no farther"—"So long and no longer"—"I'll do this, but not that." As long as we're not tested in certain areas, we can work within a "designer" commitment, customized to fit all our personal fears.

We knew this move would take trust, complete trust. We would have to give up the businesses, our only means of support. We would be totally dependent on the Lord to provide our food, our clothing—everything.

Yes, we knew that when we died we'd be in heaven with Jesus, but from this point on, we chose to take whatever remaining time God granted us and live as if we had died to ourselves that day. We wanted to live new, not just as nice people, but in doing all that we could to advance the kingdom of God.

How would we go about this? Would our iron be tested by fire? Were we full of faith or was it ignorance? Where would we start? We didn't realize at the time that the real question was not, "Where would we start?" but, "Where would we stop?"

3

VISIONS AND DREAMS

Sondra and I made the decision to live our lives as if they had ended and begun again—this time to accomplish whatever God wanted, whatever He needed us to do. We asked the Lord to use us. Within weeks we were filled with excitement over an idea—an idea to get a ship, and then staff it with volunteers, load it with food, clothes and medicine and deliver it all to needy people. A giant fantasy? An impossible dream?

We paid a visit to Agnes Numer, a wonderful woman of God who lives on a ranch in Palmdale, California. Agnes is an elderly lady, a longtime friend of my mother and mine. Years ago, God told Agnes to "put on her tennis shoes and run" and she is doing that until this day. She uses her home, Somerhaven Ranch, as a missionary training base, as well as operating a large-scale food and supply distribution program for the poor.

My mother and Agnes had been praying for me throughout the years and during our visit, Agnes prayed with us both. The Lord spoke to our hearts, saying that my dreams were not my own but His. He made reference to a ship, as if its existence was a foregone conclusion. He told me to keep my eyes on Him. "Do not look at the circumstances. Do not look to the right nor the left, but keep your eyes straight on me. As the captain keeps a ship's log, there will also be a 'Lord's log', a record of the things that I am doing."

We have kept the Lord's log, a daily record of the many miracles—the basis for this book.

One thing I knew for sure, if we were going to get a ship, it would have to be a miracle! We were in the process of expanding our horse operations and, although business was good, cash on hand was short. We had established a nonprofit charity (it was good for business) as an offshoot of our Park West Polo and Hunt Club. But since it had always been our policy to spend the money collected at fund-raisers on the immediate project at hand, the Park West Children's Fund account had a balance of $38.

Sondra and I began our search for a ship in San Diego, California, where many tuna boats were being sold. We were thrilled at the sight and size of the 10th Street terminal fleet. It was there that we first stepped aboard a vessel as potential owners. The experience was challenging because we knew so very little about ships.

I had been to "sea" one time as a young man—a twenty-six mile trip to Catalina Island on a $6 ferry boat ride. Later I got a forty foot yacht, a beautiful, clean Cris Craft Constellation docked in Marina Del Rey. It was a great boat for cocktail parties or having friends over as she sat tied to the dock, but because of my inexperience I had never taken her out. If anyone asked for a cruise, we would make excuses so we wouldn't have to leave the safety of the berth.

One day, there was a gentle breeze and the weather seemed perfect. I sat up in my captain's chair, wheel in hand, watching big yachts filled with people going by—yachts being steered by bald headed, cigar-smoking guys holding cocktail glasses in one hand while steering with the other. I looked at these men and a craziness came over me. *Surely if they can do it, I can do it.*

Some of the boys who worked at the polo club were relaxing on deck. On an impulse I hit the starter buttons, and both engines came alive with a roar. I hollered down to my salty crew, "Cast off all lines, mateys! We're going to sea!"

They scrambled to undo the ropes and away we went. We cruised slowly by some of the biggest yachts in the country. Their skippers dipped their caps as we raised our glasses and cruised by. *This,* I thought, *is a piece of cake.*

We were nearing the end of Sea Basin, where all the biggest yachts were moored. Across the end of the basin was the biggest boat in the harbor.

I had watched other rich dudes make this maneuver many times. Our boat was a twin engine so I took both throttles in hand, confident in my abilities. Bringing one throttle back hard, I took the other throttle and thrust it forward, knowing this would cause the boat to pivot and turn around. Evidently, however, I did something wrong because both engines coughed and quit. I don't know what happened but the boat felt like it picked up speed and it was imminent that we were going to broadside that grand yacht dead ahead of us. It's funny the thoughts that run through your mind at times like this. As I tried frantically to restart the boat I thought, *I'll throw my body between the boats and try to act as a cushion, or I could jump off the back, swim underwater to shore and say I was never there.*

I wasn't serving the Lord at the time, but I began to pray, *Lord, help me! Save me! I'm at the edge of financial ruin. Help me get this boat back to shore safely and I'll never untie it again. I'll sell it or something.*

Just about then, one of the engines started. I put it into reverse and the boat just sat there and went round and round backwards. Finally, a good Samaritan passed by in a small boat. He came aboard and helped me bring the boat back to the dock. I never untied that yacht again until it was sold, deciding instead to stick with horses. They were kinder to me and much easier to control.

This shows beyond a doubt that the Lord didn't pick me to head up a ship organization because of my vast nautical expertise. I couldn't even steer a boat! My only real qualification was that I was **willing**.

As we toured various ships for sale, I didn't even know what questions to ask. Escorted by marine brokers, we walked through huge ships, knowing their value was in the millions of dollars, and knowing we had no realistic ability to purchase them. Still, we felt it was our job to proceed with the plan; it was the Lord's job to finance it. So we continued to struggle our way through the showings, picking up more information with each new ship.

In late September, we got a call from a broker named Chris whom we had met aboard a ship named "El Cid" in San Diego. Chris said that he had heard from a man in Tacoma, Washington, who worked for an engine repair firm. They were selling a ship they had held onto as an investment for the past eight years.

It was necessary now to relocate the vessel. It was not under its own power and would have to be towed. The owners hadn't found a new berth and it was costing thousands of dollars a month just to moor and maintain it. It was an ideal time to sell her; Chris said he was sure that they would now be entertaining bids. Thinking the ship would be good for our purposes, he suggested we fly up to Washington to check into it.

We called Tacoma and set up an appointment with Bill Walker, president of the company that owned the vessel, and with his general manager, John Rickabaugh. We asked John if he thought the company might be interested in donating the ship. That wasn't something they'd even thought of considering, he said, and he certainly didn't think so, but we were welcome to approach Mr. Walker on it if we'd like. That night we flew into Tacoma and checked into our hotel to wait anxiously for the next morning's meeting.

At nine a.m. we met with John Rickabaugh and went to see the ship. Arriving at the dock alongside the ship, we got our first look at the vessel.

We were astounded by her size! She was forty feet longer than a football field, fifty feet wide and seven stories high from top to bottom! The ship looked like a floating island and we suddenly realized that the Lord may be thinking bigger than we were.

We got out of the car and followed the men up a wooden ladder that lay alongside the hull. The outside steel had great sheets of paint peeling down her side. She hadn't been properly maintained in thirty years but, in spite of this, the ship was beautiful to us. We reached the decks and surveyed them. She sure was rusty, but she was big and exciting! Was there a chance this vessel could become ours? Could this be the one, Lord?

The generators could not be activated, so by flashlight our guides took us to the bridge, galley, staterooms, cargo holds and engine room. It was difficult to see but, still, our enthusiasm grew. We were feeling joy and great excitement! She was big, ocean going, carried 5,000 tons of cargo and her holds were refrigerated.

The ship slept fifty, the main engine was fuel efficient and four auxiliary generators were available for plenty of power. We could light up a small city with the generators on this ship!

Oh sure, there were problems. She was missing parts, the main engine injectors and more. But even the sight of the completely barren wheelhouse didn't discourage us. All the equipment had either been stolen or sold. Everything—no wheel, no stanchion, no compass, no telegraph, no electronics, no radios—nothing— only wires hanging from the ceiling where lights used to be and cables coming up through the floor where something used to be. Even the knobs on the doors had been pilfered! We could see there was much work to be done. Still, to us, the ship was majestic. Nothing could have dulled her beauty in our eyes.

But wait, we had to get a grip on reality here. We hadn't even talked to the owner and besides, his man John didn't think he'd go for a donation. We certainly couldn't afford to pay what the ship was worth.

We followed the men back to their office to meet with Bill Walker and to see what the Lord had in mind.

Bill was a polite businessman, keenly interested in the story I told him about a ship to carry supplies to needy people. I told him about the Polo Club and the Park West Children's Fund (our tax-exempt organization), showed him pictures of the parties, programs and events we had hosted and then quickly shared what was on our hearts. I spoke to Bill about twenty minutes. Then he paused to evaluate what I'd told him, and we silently prayed, hoping he'd say he'd think about it.

After another moment of thought, Bill looked at me and said, "Meet me at my lawyer's tomorrow, Don. I'll give you the ship, free and clear. There's not so much as a cigarette butt against her."

So there we were, the owners of a ship, 100% debt free! In honor to the Lord, we decided to name her "Spirit." The miracles had begun!

The Spirit Ship when we saw her in 1985 and mid-way through restoration (bottom)

4

A SHIP BOUND FOR GOD'S GLORY

In our great zeal, we failed to realize that restoring this vessel was a massive and almost impossible task. Agnes Numer was one of the few people we knew who didn't think we'd gone mad. When we told her that the Lord had given us the ship and that we'd put out a call for helpers, she responded by sending us five of her best workers.

On October 5, 1985, we arrived in Tacoma and took a close look at the vessel, now totally ours. We actually owned a **ship**, an old, rusty, seven-story high monster that had sat in salt water and had been neglected and vandalized for thirty years. As we gazed at her in amazement, somehow it seemed as if the ship had increased in size several times over since last we saw her.

Life with Spirit was rough, and from the day we arrived the pressure cooker was on. The owners of the dock at which we were moored had offered our space to someone else as of October 1 (someone who was willing to pay $5,000 a month). So, when we signed ownership papers on October 2, the owners of the dock ordered us to move immediately. This request was the first of the "impossible" tasks connected to the restoration of Spirit. Needless to say, it's rather difficult to move a 4,000 ton, seven-story vessel that hasn't been to sea in thirty years—especially when we had no place to put her and no money to pay for moorage even if we found a space!

We spent the first few days aboard climbing from one end of the ship to the other, investigating what we had (and what we did not have), and evaluating the overwhelming job ahead. Still, in our great ignorance, we thought we could reactivate the Spirit in a couple of months. Paul Dean, a prestigious writer for the *Los Angeles Times*, came to Tacoma to write a story about what we were doing and had quite a laugh when we explained, "We hope to be at sea by Christmas."

Many people heard what we were doing and came to visit. Some were people with great expertise in the maritime field. Many were Christians, but some were not. We started to hear rumors about the condition of the ship. Some said it would take seven to ten million dollars to replace all the broken and missing equipment and activate all systems—that is, if we could find parts. The vessel was forty-one years old and suitable parts were rare. Also, the word was out that the bottom of the ship was probably rotten. Most people simply shook their heads and said we were wasting our time, that Spirit would never go back to sea.

Our guests asked endless questions. How could we afford to take her into dry dock? Where would we get five thousand tons of supplies? How would we make sure when we delivered the goods that they wouldn't be pillaged by black market criminals or confiscated by foreign governments? How could we pay all the port fees overseas (and here in the U.S.)? What about the labor costs for dock workers? Where did we intend to get our crew and how were we going to feed them? What about ship's officers? Surely we weren't expecting them to volunteer!

And did we actually think that fuel companies would provide fuel for free? What about the poor people in the U.S.? Did we intend to sail off with the goods that rightfully belonged to them, giving the supplies away to strangers in foreign lands? What organization was backing us? Where was our support? To whom did we report? Who was our spiritual covering? What denomination would give us their stamp of approval? What made us think that God Almighty would be so foolish as to choose people like us for this job when there were so many others who were far, far more qualified?

The questions overwhelmed us. (Granted, there was something about the sight of that barren wheelhouse that could easily make people think we were truly out of touch with reality or maybe even crazy.)

The discouragement hardest to shake came from well-meaning pastors who came aboard and compassionately explained to us (immature Christians) how we had stepped out ahead of God. They would deliver their message in a kind way, carefully trying not to imply that we were absolute fools. Some would tell us we should act quickly, sell the ship while there was still time, return to our profitable business, join a neighborhood church, and put ourselves into the hands of a pastor who would show us the road that would best serve the purpose of the Lord. They explained that with guidance from a man of God, we would come to understand the true nature of our calling and be directed to the proper path. Through years of studying Scripture, we would learn the wisdom of not making such presumptuous mistakes.

All these words pierced like the claws of a dragon. We loved God so much and wanted to serve Him with our lives, but we began to see that some men didn't evaluate our decision in that light. We realized right away that we could not look to people for moral support and we were careful not to even mention the subject of financial support to avoid the risk of incurring any further wrath.

I had to fly back to Los Angeles on business for a few days as I had not yet liquidated the last of the ranches. The night before I returned to the ship, I received a call from one of the crew in Tacoma. The entire crew had been praying and felt confirmation that they had received a word from the Lord. "The Spirit is only usable for scrap parts," the crewman said, "too many things missing, too much work." Another ship would be the one we'd sail.

I listened to his report and hung up, sick to my stomach. We greatly respected our friends on the ship, admired their relationships with the Lord and their communion with Him. But I couldn't believe what they were telling me was true. Life was hard on the ship. We were living with no power, no lights, no heat, no running water, no toilets, hard cold steel and many skeptical visitors. Maybe the crew was just discouraged or maybe they *were* hearing from God.

Sleep didn't come to me that night. In the morning, the Lord spoke to my heart in no uncertain terms, giving me undeniable orders. I had heard direct words from the Lord before but nothing so definite, so powerful and unconditional as this. "Do not look to the right or the left. Do not look at the circumstances but go directly forward. Be strong, be steadfast; I will make the way. It is a **new thing** I do."

I returned to Tacoma and told the crew what the Lord had said to me. Everyone was encouraged, and we spent that day chipping, sanding, cleaning and washing the decks.

As though confirming God's words, almost immediately the crew was able to set up a route of grocers and farms where we could collect surplus food items. In this way, we were able to provide the food needs for the crew. In addition, we started distributing excess food to local feeding programs.

As the days wore on, we continually looked for an affordable spot where we could moor Spirit. It was now almost the end of October and the owners of our dock were impatient. We wanted to be downtown at the Port of Seattle. Our thought was that the ship would get more exposure there, possibly resulting in some help from the public. It was then that the reality of owning a ship began to sink in. We learned that dock fees at the Port of Seattle were $511 a day—every day—Saturdays, Sundays, holidays, every day of every month. And then there was the matter of a tugboat tow from Tacoma to Seattle. Three tugs would be needed to do the job and that would cost thousands of dollars.

A local tugboat captain offered to help us find moorage. He told us about a shipyard at Bainbridge (a small island across the bay from Seattle), that would let us anchor just offshore for $600 a month. We didn't know anything about Bainbridge Island and didn't want to go there, but we hadn't much choice.

The local tugboat captain's response was discouraging when we asked if he thought a tugboat company might help us move for free. He laughed and explained how with a ship this size, dead in the water, you need one of the large companies like Crowley Maritime to do the job, but those companies didn't donate. "Why should they?" he said. "After all, they're the best. Forget it. Pull out your checkbook." (I soon learned to live with the public's constant misconception that I had a huge bankroll somewhere that I was reluctant to use. I guess they assumed that no one would be crazy enough to take on this project without a chunk of money stashed somewhere.)

We opened the local phone book to find the telephone number of some tug companies, called one after another and asked if they would consider towing our ship from Tacoma to Bainbridge Island for free. When we called Crowley Maritime, they asked us to bring by a letter and some material about Park West and they would review it. We put something together as quickly as possible and that evening drove to the main office in Seattle to leave the packet with the night watchman.

We prayed fervently. The owners of the dock in Tacoma were threatening to sue us and we had to get the ship out of there. We didn't have the cash to pay for the tow and our only hope was that hearts in this big building would be touched by the Lord.

The next afternoon, a woman called from Crowley Maritime to say that they had decided to take the job free—not a dime would be charged for this big service! A few days later, the "Hercules" and two other friendly tugs came and hooked onto the Spirit. As we threw off the lines, it was a great moment for the vessel. She was on the move!

Our new spot in Winslow on Bainbridge Island at Russ Trask Shipyard was a ferry ride across Puget Sound from the big city, in an isolated harbor located right next to the State of Washington ferry maintenance yard. This site turned out to be a pleasant surprise.

Eagle Harbor was tiny but exquisite! We had no idea how

beautiful a place it was until we arrived. With pine trees down to the water's edge, Canadian geese flying over our decks then swooping down into the water beside us, mallard ducks everywhere we looked, it was incomparable! Looking out each of the ship's portholes, it was as if we were gazing upon a stunning master's painting. We continued to have an eye on downtown Seattle but, in the meantime, we had great natural beauty and the privacy we needed to make some early mistakes without the scrutiny of the public eye.

Anchorage at Russ Trask Shipyard brought new challenges. We were offshore, tied to phone poles, called pilings, driven into the water. (These poles stabilized the movement of the ship on the water.) We had no way to reach the vessel except by rowboat and we had to haul water from the city. Our men would row some empty five-gallon buckets ashore in an eight-foot dinghy, carry the buckets up an icy, narrow dock to the car, drive to the local service station, fill them up with water, drive back to the shipyard, haul the full buckets back a few hundred yards up the dock to put them into the dinghy, row back to the ship and pass the heavy buckets hand-to-hand up an old, decaying rope ladder that we used to come aboard. Fortunately, some time later we were able to eliminate the hauling process by running a hose underwater from a shore-side spout.

As winter set in, we began to freeze. It was one of the coldest Seattle winters in twenty years and our all-electric, seven story steel ship with no heat sat in the ice-cold waters of Puget Sound. This was a trying time for a bunch of Southern California high-desert thin bloods. The icicles on the insides of our portholes chased those on the outside. The dampness pierced every part of our beings. Moisture reached us even through the several layers of clothing we constantly wore, so we installed an old fifty-gallon oil drum in the mess hall as a wood-burning stove, cut a hole in it and stuck in a pipe to let the smoke out. Then we put the stove pipe out the porthole, threw wood in the drum and lit a match, burning anything we could get our hands on to try and keep warm.

There were twenty-two thousand gallons of diesel fuel in Spirit's tanks when she was donated, and it wasn't too long before we were able to activate an engine. Three big generators—each designed as a diesel locomotive to pull train cars—created a great deal of electricity and used a terrific amount of fuel. Each of these big generators burned 250 gallons of fuel each day so, in order to conserve fuel, we rebuilt the smaller emergency Hill generator. This provided us with some heat and electricity, eventually enabling us to activate stoves, water and toilet systems.

But the Hill didn't give us as much power as we actually needed. Electric heaters drew too much current. We had to stop welding in order to cook and stop cooking to use the water heater. Still, it burned less than one-third the fuel of the locomotive engine. At night we'd turn the generator off and then start it in the morning before dawn. In this way, we were able to stretch and conserve our limited supply of fuel. Then we started to pursue donations, not of money, but of items we needed to refit the ship.

Out of curiosity, we looked into the ship's history. The Spirit had been built in 1944 by Pennsylvania Shipyard in Beaumont, Texas, and had been commissioned by the navy. She carried supplies to the troops overseas, transported returning servicemen home and successfully dodged the Japanese Navy, who, on several occasions, hunted Spirit to destroy her. In 1946, Spirit's military career ended and she was decommissioned. Alaska Steamship Company leased her from the government and she was employed for several years to haul refrigerated cargo from Puget Sound to Nome, Alaska. In 1957, the Spirit made her last commercial voyage, and she was later purchased by Bill Walker.

As November came and went, the Spirit began to come alive, and before long it was as if a heartbeat had returned to the ship.

Volunteers of every kind signed on to serve as crew, many of whom (we were to discover) were rebels. At first, it was our policy to accept as crew anyone who asked to come aboard if they didn't seem dangerous or too crazy.

We tried to show love to each one, but it was often difficult.

We now had an "official" chief engineer and, although we were grateful to have his help, he was not a Christian man and didn't understand us or our unusual priorities. He was critical and made continual negative comments on the condition of the ship and our lack of experience. His attitude began to discourage our tiny crew, which was the last thing we needed.

Another member of the crew claimed he had hurt himself and just stayed in his room all day. We were suspicious that he was smoking pot and we knew for certain he got drunk every couple of days. Then there was the French Canadian chef who had witnessed a murder and was using the ship to hide out. He was an excellent cook but seldom sober.

After the article by Paul Dean in the *Los Angeles Times* was published in November, Dick Clark Productions asked to meet with us regarding the production of a Movie of the Week based on what they had read in the *Times*. It was an enticing thought. They sent us an extensive folder about themselves and their abilities, including a very impressive dossier on directors and producers who worked with them. Although it seemed to us quite premature, we decided to meet with them. However, we soon realized that their intention was to give all the credit for this project to **us**. This was not acceptable. No one knew better than we did that we were merely passengers on a ship bound for God's glory. Incredibly, over the next few months, we were extended **seven** similar invitations to produce feature films or television movies of the week. We politely declined each one.

We received several strange phone calls following the publication of the *L.A. Times* article. One particularly memorable call came from a man who was convinced that I was a spirit from outer space, not merely a human being but what he called a "walk-in." By this we learned that he meant some sort of advanced spirit that inhabits the bodies of humans in order to bring goodwill to the earth. This sort of foolishness took many forms.

Eventually, more mature Christians came to join with our small original band of pioneers. Sondra's brother Ray George had decided to give up his accounting job in San Diego and join us early the next year. I felt in my spirit that he would be in charge of the food operations. Ray arrived in February and, almost immediately upon his arrival, that aspect of our project blossomed. He worked very hard, bringing in great amounts of choice groceries. His diligence, respect and appreciation for the donations caused the food outreach to flourish.

In April of our first year, a young man from Texas, Jamie Saunders, and his pregnant wife Debi moved aboard the ship. I was excited about Jamie from the start and as the months passed, he became a tremendous asset to our mission. He served not only as a minister, wise and knowledgeable in Scripture, but also as a mechanical and inventive genius. No problem stumped him for long, and his uplifting, quiet manner was an inspiration to us all. Jamie had an unusual, steadfast commitment to the project because some years before we'd met, the Lord had shown him that in the last days He would help develop "major offenses" for the gospel on the earth, one of those being ships. Jamie felt sure that our fledgling ship ministry (later to be known as "Friend Ships") was one of those major offenses.

Thus, Jamie had a rock-solid commitment to this dream. He placed himself under my authority, even though I was not very knowledgeable in spiritual things and wasn't the leader that many people thought I should be. Jamie knew I was young in the Lord, but he believed and trusted in his God and in the Scriptures, and he tolerated me, knowing I had miles to go. For this we were extremely grateful.

Many other wonderful friends came to join us. It was a mystery (that only God understood) as to why anyone would be willing to uproot their life to pursue this impossible dream and join with us through tough times to fulfill it. Throughout the refit of Spirit, in spite of our band of maritime novices, we never had a serious accident—even though shipyard repair is one of the highest risk occupations in the world. We were protected by the blood of Jesus.

For many months, the crew struggled when boarding the ship. Our only access was by way of that old, decaying rope ladder that hung down the side. Later we used some long planks as a gangway and nailed strips of wood across so we wouldn't slip or fall on our way down. But the planks were very steep and, when coated with ice or snow, the gangway was like a ski run.

Obviously, it was difficult to get on and off the ship safely. At the bottom of the slope were the icy waters of Puget Sound, so we thought maybe we should purchase a gangway. However, we found out that the forty-foot aluminum ones (with self-adjusting steps for the change in tide level) sold for $25,000 each. We started praying for a proper gangway. A few weeks later Jamie and I saw some rusty lifeboat-lifting apparatus called davits lying in the yard of a local maritime school. We went to speak to the head instructor.

He said to wait a few minutes until his class was out and he would talk further to us. We walked down and talked to the yard supervisor about the davits and asked what were they going to do with them? He gruffly replied, "Well if you think the school would give them to you, you're mistaken. This college doesn't give anything away. It's valuable metal and they'll sell it by the pound for scrap."

As we waited for the instructor, we peered into a shed with lots of maritime ropes, brackets, parts and other nautical items. We also saw two large gangways, both about forty feet long. One was broken but solid—possibly usable with some repair. The other one hanging just above it was brand new, one of those $25,000 jobs.

The instructor came out and greeted us. We said, "If you're throwing those old metal lifting davits away, do you think we might have them?"

He said, "No, those have been sold for scrap and the man is coming to pick them up. Sorry I can't help you." We thanked him and turned to walk away, but the man called us back: "I have something else if you're interested. I have a spare gangway hanging up in the shed."

I said, "Oh, great!" Then, almost jokingly, "Which one?" "The one up above."

"Say that again," I said.

"The aluminum one with the swivel steps, the big one up there, the new one." He indicated the gangway I had been admiring.

We couldn't believe our eyes or ears. The gangway we had prayed for was hanging on the wall before us. I turned to the schoolmaster, excited. "I'm sorry, please forgive me," I said. "But you are going to have to walk over and put your hand on the one you're talking about."

He headed straight for the brand new $25,000 gangway and laid his hand on it. "But," he said, "you've got to take it immediately. Bring your truck and pick it up today."

We didn't have a truck so we went straight to a U-Haul truck rental and explained our good fortune to the manager. We were out of cash and told him we had no money to rent a truck. The man, laughing and quite amused, started out to the back lot and told us to follow. He led us to a big, fine truck, handed us the keys and told us to try not to have too much fun! We hopped in and drove straight back to the school where the grouchy yard supervisor sat on his forklift waiting for us to return so he could give us the gangway and go home. "I told you they wouldn't give you those rusty old davits. They don't give away anything around here," he said in a no-joke manner as he loaded the gangway into our truck with his forklift. Jamie and I looked at each other, incredulous. It was as if the man was wearing blinders and couldn't see that he was loading the most expensive item in the yard! We waved good-bye to him as we drove away, praising the Lord all the way home!

As God had revealed to me, Ray was successful with the food ministry right from the beginning. In one week, we were able to establish ongoing sources of fruit, vegetables, bread, sweets, dairy products and even flowers. So much was the provision that we were able to supply five feeding programs that first week alone and, as the months passed, Ray continued to build the route. He delivered food to the Salvation Army, the Food Bank and a home for the mentally ill.

We found the maritime community warm and generous! Helpful men, who knew where all the bargains were, could tell us where to go for a straight deal and which places to avoid.

We made a great effort to make friends with the church and charity community of Bainbridge, but still, strange stories about us circulated. A new arrival at the ship attended a local church and was informed that we were "humanists." A mission we were helping held a meeting of local agencies and told them that the crew of the Spirit was a band of "neo-Nazis" and "followers of Rajneesh." Try as we would to be loving and friendly, we were locked into our lonely isolation.

So, we kept our heads down and continued to work day after day on the tedious task of preparing the ship for sea. As we worked at chipping away the old and peeling paint, the Lord was chipping away on our hearts.

Don Tipton

Sondra Tipton

5

JUST A CHEESEBURGER

We began to realize that it was going to take us much longer than we had ever thought to prepare this ship for world missions. Everything we thought would take a day to fix actually took weeks. Everything we thought would take weeks took months. And then it dawned on me: God wasn't resurrecting an old vessel, *we* were the resurrection. He was after us, from the inside out. Nothing seems to mean more to God then the ability to get to the hearts of His people. Here we were, caught working on this old bucket, as He worked on us, His "vessels."

Sondra's February birthday approached, during our first year on this ship project, so I asked her what she wanted for her birthday. Without hesitation, she answered, "A cheeseburger." We had been on a steady diet of donated vegetables and bakery products, and the thought of a cheeseburger sounded good to her. But I had no money. Suddenly, the realization came over me that with all the things I had done in my life, with all the positions I'd held, the people I knew and the money I'd made, I now couldn't even afford to buy my wife a cheeseburger for her birthday.

On top of that, the ship was running out of provisions. It seemed inevitable that people would soon have to return home. Months of freezing temperatures, no showers, troublesome volunteers, discouraging visitors and attacks on our character seemed to culminate at that moment in Sondra as she burst into tears.

In anguish, I sought the Lord. *We're just barely staying alive out here, almost freezing to death and making very little progress on the ship. Everybody tells me this ship will never sail. I've got no financial support, we've got no parts, no fuel, no crew members who know anything about ships except the engineer and he tells visitors and volunteers how ignorant I am and how useless our efforts here are!*

Were we ready to give up? No! *In spite of everything, Lord, we believe You sent us here and we're staying. If everybody goes home and the ship sinks to the bottom of the bay, Sondra and I will climb to the top of the crow's nest and cry out to You until You raise this ship back up. There is not an army tough enough or a baseball bat big enough to get us to leave this ship. We're here to stay.*

That desperate prayer of affirmation proved later to mark a major turning point. After that night, the windows of heaven opened and God abundantly blessed us with everything we needed to forge ahead.

Periodically, we shopped for parts at the Navy Dump Yard in Bremerton. It was the only place we could buy what we needed at scrap prices, so we visited there as often as we could. Our neighbors at the ferry maintenance yard allowed us to crawl through their dumpsters searching for items they had thrown away. Many of these prizes, such as pipe fittings and electrical wires, still had lots of life left in them. At a government auction, we were able to purchase twenty-two hospital beds for a dollar apiece, thus securing our very first medical cargo.

Every week we had been calling Jan Kelly, manager of marine operations at the Port of Seattle, asking if a spot had become available for Spirit to dock. And every week Mr. Kelly said to call back on Monday. One day in August, I felt very strongly that we should go straight to Seattle and meet with him. I told Sondra to get ready, we were catching the next ferry into the city.

When we arrived at the port building, we asked for and were introduced to Mr. Kelly, who was obviously busy and not ready to receive guests. Still, he was gracious and invited us in.

As I apologized for barging in on him and explained our circumstances, Sondra prayed silently. Jan listened closely to my story then quietly replied, "You can bring the Spirit into Pier 66 at the beginning of next month," I couldn't believe my ears! Pier 66 was right next to the port administration building.

Then he showed us his book of rates. For a ship the size of the Spirit, the official rate was over $500 a day. But Jan said the port would agree to allow us to come in for $500 a month. That was $100 less than we were paying at Bainbridge Island! With this news, there was a renewed vigor on the ship. God had just manifested Himself to us in a powerful way!

We were very excited about moving to our new dock. The whole crew felt invigorated. All of us wanted everything to be just perfect. We had only three weeks to chip and paint the hull in order to sail into Seattle on the first of September looking good. A major drive began to get the hull painted before the move. Soon everyone showed fatigue, tempers ran high. Some believed I was pushing too hard, but when I backed off, the men continued to push themselves. Even one of the crew members who wouldn't work two hours in a row when he first arrived was out on deck until after midnight, hanging over the side and chipping.

We needed more deck-chipping tools in order to keep everyone working, but of course we had no money to buy any. Our ingenious crew member Jamie came up with an idea to take some Weed Eaters that were donated and replace the cord on them with chain. Then, when we turned them on and aimed them against the hull, the rotating chain chipped at the old paint like hundreds of little hammers.

We wrote a letter to request a donation of a special metal rust preventative that retails for over $7 an ounce, asking the manufacturer if they might be interested in experimenting on a marine application and they said "yes." The company shipped us 200 gallons to prime the hull!

Again, our bank account was down. The balance stood at

$38, but the provisions were flowing and Crowley Maritime agreed to tow us for free.

As we worked that month in preparation to go to Seattle, I prayed with great expectation for the small sum of $500 so we could pay Mr. Kelly upon arrival. The month disappeared and my stomach churned. *Lord, how can I pay this bill?* While everyone was joyously praising God, I kept the situation about the lack of money to myself.

Two beautiful tugs pulled up alongside Spirit one morning at seven a.m. to take us to Seattle. As the ship was backing away from the pilings, Claudia, an old friend who lived on Bainbridge Island, ran to the shore and waved, hoping to catch a ride to Seattle with us and the rest of the volunteers and visitors who wanted to be part of this great miracle.

A small boat passed by and offered her a ride out to our ship. We dropped the ladder down the side of our hull and she bravely climbed aboard the moving ship.

We watched as the island disappeared and Seattle came closer on the horizon. In the distance, our berth was in sight. People were holding hands and singing songs. As we came in close to Seattle, I searched the docks for Mr. Kelly with my stomach in knots. What was I to say? What was I to do?

As we arrived at the docks, Mr. Kelly was nowhere in sight. The tugboats left and the gangway went down. As the cheering subsided, all the visitors began to leave. I looked down to see Claudia waving to me from the dock. She called out, "I almost forgot. My husband gave me a donation to give to you." Running back up the gangway, she presented us with a $600 check!

First, the miracle of getting the moorage, and then the payment for it in advance—both are beautiful examples of how God was always ahead of us, His provision always with us. Everyone else had enjoyed the trip to Seattle while I had fretted and worried, not knowing that the provision had been with me all along. To trust Him should be a lesson I've learned well, but somehow it has escaped me over and over again.

Shortly after we arrived in Seattle, we met a young street minister by the name of Jay, who shared a vision he received months earlier. It is one I will never forget.

Before the Spirit ship had come to Seattle, Jay had been standing on an upper floor of the Edgewater Hotel at Pier 67, next to what was to become our berth. Suddenly in his vision he was caught up and saw a tiny beam of light emanating from the surface of the water at Berth 66. It appeared to get stronger and brighter as he stared. The light became so bright that it burst forward like a nuclear explosion. Fingers of light raced across the water and across oceans to foreign lands. He saw their officials standing by the edge of the water trying to hold back the light. It passed the officials by with such energy, it flattened them. They couldn't withstand the light. It raced over the mountains and through the valleys, and people were on their knees, praising and worshipping and giving thanks to God.

Jay had no concept of what the vision meant at the time it was given to him. But one day, months later, he saw an old ship tied to the dock in the very spot from which the light had come forth. Someone told him of the ship's intended missions, and Jay realized that the light he had seen, emanated from that ship, the Spirit. It was a vision of what was to come.

We continued restoring the ship in Seattle. Financially, we were always on the edge but, even so, things never slowed down. We gave tours to hundreds of guests each month, most of whom just wanted to see the insides of an old World War II ship.

Late one summer night in Seattle we unknowingly hosted an uninvited guest. It was unusually humid and hot. The moon shone bright that night, a strange evening for the Pacific Northwest. The Spirit was rising and falling restlessly in her berth, rocking away from the dock and coming back with a bump. The gangway creaked with each rise and fall of the waves.

Wes, our photographer, had been up late working and found it hard to sleep. Thinking he heard footsteps on the gangway, he rose from his bunk to look out the porthole and saw a large man slipping quietly down the gangway, Wes' new camera in hand. It was his only camera, one he highly prized. "Stop, stop thief!" he hollered out. "Come back with my camera!" He jumped out of his bunk and ran into the passageway, one leg in his pants, one shoe in his hand, dancing around on the deck trying to locate his foot. Running down the hallway, he pushed open the hatchway door as he screamed, "Come back, come back with my camera!"

Leaping across the deck toward the gangway, bounding across the plank with only a few strides, he ran down the steps, reached the dock and dashed for the sidewalk. The streets were empty and dark, illuminated only by the moon and sparse street lighting. Skinny and wiry but in good shape for the long chase, Wes spotted the thief in the distance and took off after the large man as he ran down Alaskan Way. The chase was on. The duo ran past Pier 67, Pier 68, Pier 69, Pier 70, past parking lots.

Wes closed in on the man with each stride. The thief's legs grew weaker and Wes knew he had him then. He thought, *Dear God! What happens when I catch him? He might kill me.* The man stopped and held onto the fence, completely out of oxygen, gasping for air. Wes stopped. The thief warned him to come no closer.

Wes had no intention of going any closer. Each time the man took a step forward or backward, Wes made an adjustment and didn't let the thief come closer or go further away. He pleaded with the thief, "This is my only camera. I'm a photographer and a missionary. I work for the Lord. Our work is to help the poor and the hungry. Can't you find it in your heart to return this camera? For the Lord's work?"

The man thought for a moment and said, "This is a valuable camera. How much will you pay me for it?" Wes answered, "I don't have any money. I can't buy it." The thief then asked, "Well, what do you have to trade me for it?"

Wes gave him a quick answer without a second thought: "I have lots of food and clothes. If you come back to the ship, I'll give you boxes of food and I'll drive you to where you need to go." Wes became braver now and moved a little closer.

The big man replied, "If I come back there, you'll have me put in jail."

Wes pleaded with him. "Trust me; I'm a missionary. I wouldn't lie to you. I'm a Christian. I give you my word. I won't report you to the police if you'll just give me back my camera."

Finally, the man agreed and they walked back to the ship, the thief still holding onto the camera. Wes took him through the galley and boxed up all the food the thief selected, as well as a sack of clothes for the man and his family. They carried the food and clothing down the gangway to Wes' car. The man returned the camera to Wes, happy with Wes' Christian honesty.

As the thief turned to leave, he made this stunning announcement. "I myself am traveling with a gospel band, and as thanks for you not turning me into the sheriff, I'm gonna bring my group over to entertain your ship. We do singing and hand-clapping Southern style."

He never showed up for the meeting. (We figured that he had probably been caught and jailed on another caper.)

Another interesting guest gave us a quite a surprise and taught us an important lesson. Ray came to us one afternoon and told us that he heard that the Buddhist Temple, five miles away, needed food. We were collecting so much food that we had lots of overages and Ray wanted to know if it would be okay to share some of it with the Buddhists. We said sure. Tell them, "It comes from our Lord Jesus. " This is a great opportunity, we thought. So, for some months, Ray delivered food to the Buddhist Temple.

Then one day Ray came in with a strange request. The temple wanted to send a young lady to the ship to work for a day, as a thanks to us for our kindness. We thought, *Oh wonderful, a genuine heathen, a real chance to show her how Christians, hardened missionaries full of steel, do things. We'll show her what real Christianity is, people who can stand up under adversity.*

Usually when people come to help us, we feed them, take them on a tour, tell them about the miracles and then they encourage us with their own spiritual stories. Often by that time, we're all excited and there is little time left for work.

Instead, this Buddhist, a petite and pretty young girl with long hair, walked five miles from the temple to the ship. She bowed to everybody in her Buddhist way, hands clapped to her forehead, and presented herself for work.

We asked her, "Would you like breakfast?" "No, I've not come to eat, I've come to work," she said. "Oh," we replied, "can we give you a tour of the ship?" "No," she answered as she graciously bowed. "I've not come to tour the ship. I've come to work."

We thought this pretty strange and decided to keep a good eye on her to see what she did. We gave her a hard job to see how she reacted, taking her to the galley and giving her the job of cleaning and restacking all of the lower shelves. Needing no instructions, she got down on her knees and started pulling everything out of the cabinets. She cleaned each counter and cabinet meticulously, paying close attention to every detail.

The crew played loud blaring Christian music in the galley while she worked and walked by the galley pronouncing loud, brassy Christian slogans and praying at every opportunity in loud voices, hoping to impress her with the gospel.

Each time we came to ask her if she needed something or if we could help her in some way, she would rise, bow and say, "No thank you, I've just come to serve you," and would then continue with her work. When she was done, the galley sparkled and the cabinets were perfectly clean and neat. The young Buddhist bowed and left without a word.

Later that day, Ray went to a bakery shop on his normal afternoon food pick-ups. The man working there said to wait because he had another box for us. Leaning behind the counter, he pulled out a large box of assorted items.

Looking into the box, Ray said, "These are just the things we need, the things we don't have in our kitchen. How did you know that we need these items?"

The man told him a young Buddhist girl came in and left these items for us. It seemed she purchased them at the store and brought them to the bakery, knowing that Ray stopped there each day. She asked the owner to give the box to us but not to say where it came from. The baker offered her a ride back to the temple, a five-mile uphill walk, but she said, no, she hadn't come for a ride. She wanted only to serve the "nice crew of the Spirit Ship."

We never saw her again, but when Ray came back with his report, we listened solemnly, understanding that this young Buddhist girl had adopted many of the true values of our Lord Jesus, while not even knowing Him. Through her (and outside of our religious boundaries), we saw His principles in action, but in a better way than we who know Him often demonstrate. We felt ashamed, humbled and grateful to the Lord for giving us this profound experience. How lacking we must often appear to others.

Another very special guest that delighted us was the man who lived under a cold bridge.

One morning, after waking up under his cold steel "home", this guy peered down the hill into the bay. He had been drunk for two years. With matted hair and filthy clothes, he cried out to God, "I know I'm dying. If you don't save me God, I'm going to die. Please Lord, help me." He was hungry and some of the other drunks told him that if he went down to the old black ship at the docks, he could get food. "They never turn anyone away."

So the man, still half drunk from the night before, stumbled down to the Spirit. As we loaded him up with food, the guy asked, "What kind of ship is this that just gives food for free? I never heard of that before." We told him it was God's ship. Suddenly he decided that the Spirit ship must be the answer to his prayer. He announced, "I've got to become a crew member on this ship."

We explained that to be on the ship, he had to be sober, he had to come every morning at six a.m. to the Bible study and he had to work each day for free. In a couple of weeks, if he was still sober and clean, we would consider his application to be a crew member.

The next morning, this man known as Butch stumbled in on time for the meeting. He tried to work through the day but he was shaking pretty bad. At the end of the day he left and went back to the bridge. It was very hard for Butch to go back under that damp bridge with all of his friends who teased him and tried to pass him the bottle. They mocked him. "You'll never get to be on that ship!" But in the morning he'd get up and come back to work again, shaking less each day.

After a while, Sondra happened to ask him, "Butch, where do you stay at night?" He pointed up the hill to the old bridge and said, "I live up there, under that bridge. It has a great view of the ship." Sondra came straight to me, telling me what she'd learned. That night, Butch moved onto the ship, welcomed by a warm shower and a clean bunk.

Later we learned he had worked in the engineering department on several vessels and knew far more about ships than we did. Butch soon gave his heart to Jesus. He turned out to be one of our very best crewmen. Cleaned up and wearing new clothes, he was a surprisingly handsome man. Sometime later, a young woman, Colleen, came to the ship and became a volunteer. In time, Butch and Colleen fell in love and were married.

What a wonderful success story! Butch found Jesus, got his life back together and later took a job as an electrical construction supervisor in a large company in Alaska. He now has children, is very active in the church, continues to grow, is an asset to the community and, to this day, is full of the love of the Lord.

6

WITH GRATITUDE

The afternoon sun shone bright as Sondra and I drove over the Ballard Bridge just north of Seattle. Ballard is a fishing village with hundreds of ships. As I looked down at the many ships on the water below, one in particular struck me. The ship was sideways, out in the harbor, maneuvering back into its slip. The flying bridge, upswept bow, and fishing cockpit in the rear caught my eye. It looked like a 200 foot sports fishing yacht doing twenty knots tied to the dock. *This is the most beautiful ship I can remember seeing.* Usually I didn't take my mind off the Spirit with the thought of other ships, but this was a special case. *God must have need of a ship like this. This ship requires a closer look.*

Closer down to the water, we searched for the ship and couldn't find it. Finally we saw a small tip of her stern where she sat parked between some other vessels. Sondra and I drove over to her. We got out of the car and climbed aboard into the fishing cockpit in the rear. The excitement we felt couldn't be explained. It made no sense. Coming on a ship uninvited is like breaking into a man's house or trespassing against posted warnings, but I danced around on the back deck with my hands over my head, claiming it for Jesus. If anyone would have seen me, they would have thought for sure I was a nut.

We couldn't contact the owners, so we left word at the shipyard where she was moored that we wanted the ship and would the owner please call. No one ever replied. After some

57

months, I figured I must have temporarily lost control of my faculties. Then, out of the blue, a Christian man called the office and explained to Sondra that he had been working on a ship for a Japanese family and, although he hadn't been paid, he couldn't bring himself to leave the job because he felt the Lord had some purpose for the ship. Would we be interested in buying a new ship, he asked? Sondra explained that we didn't have funds to buy ships but sometimes people gave them to us. Then the young man mentioned the vessel's name. What a shock! Sondra recognized this as the **very** ship to which I had become so attached. She set an appointment to meet this young man along with the ship's owner.

About noon the next day, we got our first look inside the ship. It looked like a doll house; everything was so impeccable and more beautiful then we had imagined it to be. The radio room and wheelhouse looked like some sort of a spy ship with every conceivable electronic gadget. The whole ship gave the appearance that the crew had just walked off yesterday, leaving everything behind—personal slide rules, pens and pencils, pads and reading devices, wristwatches and even Japanese slippers. The drawers abounded with light bulbs, switches and spare parts.

But the young owner's story was sad. His business had fallen on hard times and he had come here to refit the vessel and try to enter American fishing waters. He had failed and lost face with his family at home—but not for his lack of trying.

I wanted the ship, but couldn't just ask him to give it to us for free. So, I thought I'd do some horse trading. I offered him a price that was less even than the value of the radio room's electronics. I knew the ship was worth much, much more.

"I'll pay you $100,000 for the ship but this is how I'll pay you. I'll offer you $10,000 a year, at the end of every year for the first five years. Then I'll give you a balloon payment of $50,000. I'll give you no down payment. I won't insure the ship and won't pay you any interest on the money. You have to give me all of the ownership papers up front, signed over to me free and clear, and just trust me."

I thought, *Now I've made my offer. He'll refuse, then I can go home and stop thinking about this ship.* But to my delight, he said, "I'll take your deal."

So he went to his attorney who had a standard purchase agreement. As he started to type in the particulars of the contract, the attorney told the man that no one in his right mind would make a deal like this. "It's the worst deal I've ever heard of," he stormed, refusing to write it up. "I'll give you the forms. You fill out what you want. Cross out all the standard stuff and initial it. I don't want anything to do with this."

So, here we were, the owners of a second ship. In great thankfulness for what the Lord had done, we decided to christen her with the name, "Gratitude."

It was shortly before Christmas and we decided to throw a birthday party for Jesus and invite hurting people. We went down to the shopping mall on the Seattle waterfront at Pier 70 and asked the owners if we could bring our new ship to the berth outside the stores. We would hang toys from Gratitude's cargo booms and set up shop for a toy and food distribution program inside their mall. They agreed and by Christmas we were flooded with beautiful toys and lots of great food to give away!

We worked hard to give out the love of Christ to the city of Seattle as our new ship Gratitude arrived at Pier 70. We put a tree with lights on her bow and false wooden bottoms two feet down in the cargo hold, filling them with toys until they were popping out of the hatches. A big cargo net, filled with balls, bats, inflatable toy animals, and a red wagon, hung from the booms above deck. The wheelhouse windows were full of stuffed animals. When we finished decorating her, the crew stood back on the dock laughing.

Seattle children came to the pier and viewed the "toy ship" with excitement before coming indoors to receive their gifts. Once inside the store, we had toys stashed in a loft where our team of crew and local church volunteers put orders together to meet the families' needs. When the supply of toys nearly disappeared, the team hollered down to the lower level. About that time we heard our truck come rumbling down the pier. We ran out to meet the truck, threw open the door and saw beautiful new toys, stuffed from floor to ceiling!

A tractor-trailer rig had recently flipped over on the highway. The company declared the toys damaged, the insurance company paid off and the company now needed to discard the product. We agreed to take the load, knowing it might be damaged beyond repair. When the new truck arrived, it was filled with stuffed animals, still in plastic wrappers inside their individual boxes in perfect shape. After all, how could you injure stuffed lions, tigers and teddy bears?

A new eighty-story skyscraper, the biggest in Seattle—the Columbia Building—sponsored a Christmas party and the entrance fee was a toy. The guests brought beautiful gifts which were presented to us to give to poor children. More than 2,000 toys showed up from the U.S. Marines' program. We helped other ministries with toys. We home delivered to shut-ins. We sent a group to a party for American Indian children, where we gave out toys, danced, sang and performed puppet shows.

Our store also featured a large nativity scene, gospel singers and a band. Volunteers came from area churches. Some told our guests about Jesus and passed out tracts, while others helped us give out two toys per child and load each family up with turkey, rice, beans, vegetables, bread and pastries! Jesus supplied it all!

As Sondra and I stood back looking at the Lord's Christmas party, we were so amazed. We had our own ship tied to this very dock with toys in the cargo hold, in the windows and hanging from nets. We had a storefront inside the mall, thousands and thousands of toys, turkey dinners and all the trimmings for any needy person who came by, no questions asked. We had people waiting in line up to three hours for their toys, groups singing, playing instruments and serenading people, volunteers with silver trays full of hot coffee and donuts, serving the people waiting in line. Christians passed out gospel tracts and witnessed about Jesus. And it all happened without one dime of investment. No one paid, nothing bought, nothing charged—storefronts, malls, a ship at the docks, food, toys and music. The celebration went on for four days in all, nonstop for anyone who came. Yes, it was truly His party in His Spirit.

A most memorable moment happened for me during that Christmas adventure. One afternoon, a somewhat embarrassed shipyard worker (recently laid off, I later learned) waited in line, hoping to get some toys for his children. This proud man who had always been able to make his own way—a welder, a ship's fitter since he was a young man—had never before needed to ask for help. But now the hard times in the maritime industry had cost him his job.

He approached the counter, obviously ashamed because he had nothing to give his children for Christmas. His family didn't even have enough food for Christmas dinner. In a quiet manner and with a soft trembling voice he asked the girls at the counter, "Why do you do this? Is it a promotional thing? Do I have to promise to buy something?"

The girls smiled at him and said, "This is our Lord's birthday, the great giver. It's the kind of party He likes to give, one where the presents belong to you."

Tears began to well up in his eyes and he tried to hold back the flow. With voice breaking he whispered, "I thought He'd forgotten me. I thought He didn't care."

Passing along with the others in line, he gathered toys for each of his children, loading his sacks full of groceries for a Christmas meal with turkey and all the trimmings. He followed the line out into the hallway where many others were waiting for their turn to come in.

For some reason, I watched him. He seemed shaken. One by one, he set his heavy packages down on the floor and slowly dropped to his knees in front of the hundreds of waiting people. Boldly and without shame, tears running down his cheeks, he raised his hands and began to thank God.

He deeply impressed me as I watched him. I couldn't help but think of the story of the ten lepers that Jesus had healed and the one who came back to give thanks. It was a lot of effort that year, many days of hard work—but when I looked at that man kneeling there on the hard wood floor, I thought, *Thank you God for my reward. To see this man and his precious heart has made it all worthwhile!*

As the toys and food were given away, I stared outside the window at our beautiful new ship. Indeed, Gratitude was a Christmas gift of love from the Father, the most beautiful ship in all Seattle. While we gave out gifts to the children, God had brought us another ship for the Kingdom!

Then, in my natural fear and lack of trust, I began to worry right away about that first $10,000 payment.

7

DOUBLE GRATITUDE

Gratitude's excellent condition meant that she could be underway within a few weeks, so we split the crew and worked on both ships at the same time. Soon we fired up Gratitude's main engine for the first time and began to pray about where the Lord wanted our first mission to be. Now we had a ship that could actually move under its own power, which was a whole new experience for us.

Gratitude had to be shifted from one pier to another, so we decided the move presented a good opportunity to take her on a sea trial. I had to be at a meeting and had an uneasy feeling about not being there for the Gratitude's move. Something in my spirit—something that I couldn't put my finger on—was wrong.

I told Sondra, "If you follow my instructions exactly, I can go to my meeting, and you and Jamie can move the ship. Listen closely. The tugboat captain coming to command the ship is used to handling small vessels of this size. If, for some reason, he doesn't show up, shut down the ship. **Don't let anyone else take command.** Several captains have requested to go along for the ride, but only this one captain is familiar with maneuvering this size ship. We're uninsured and can't risk an accident." They both agreed with the plan.

I went on to my meeting to look at yet another ship. Sondra can explain what happened next.

Sondra:

We had some trouble with the cooling on the engine and

63

were held up for an hour. Meanwhile, just as Don had said, another captain showed up and asked to go along for a ride. A third captain, who had been a rear admiral in the navy and a supreme court judge, showed up too. With three captains in the wheelhouse, Jamie and I felt secure and decided to enjoy the sea trial from the flying bridge.

We waited there for a while, expecting to depart momentarily, but nothing happened. Finally, I left Jamie on the flying bridge and headed down to the engine room to see what the delay was. While climbing down I glanced over to the crowd on the pier watching us prepare to leave. I saw the captain to whom we had assigned the command. He was standing on the dock. Shocked, I called out, "What are you doing over there?"

"I don't have anymore time, and besides, you got too much brass in there!" he shouted back.

Suddenly, without an order given to cast off the stern line, the ship pulled away from the dock. Our young crewman scrambled to loose the rope from the davit before we pulled the wharf down.

Whoever had given the command to take the ship out (and I didn't know who at this point), had ordered the helm to steer hard to port. This was absurd as we had 140 miles of unobstructed Puget Sound to back out into and negotiate a turn. Instead, he gave a direct command to the helm, hard left rudder to port, aiming the stern straight at an old fuel dock. Even worse, whoever was giving the commands never bothered to find out that the ship was not wheelhouse controlled but rather engine room controlled, which means you have to call down to the engine room and tell the engineer what speed and forward or reverse. To top it off, every control in the ship was written in Japanese.

Our engineer (who had just joined the crew) was still trying to figure out all the controls—what to pull and what to shove. It took a little extra time to make everything work. On top of that, Gratitude's main engine was an extremely powerful direct reversible, which means that it has to be shut down and started again in order to change from reverse to forward. The transition time is slow, very slow, taking more than a full minute to kick in.

In the meantime, our beautiful ship steamed headlong in reverse right toward Pier 71, the Union Oil Fuel Dock dead in its path. Jamie and I watched, horrified, realizing we were going to ram the fuel dock. We rushed to the bridge where we discovered that the rear admiral was in command. We continued to turn the vessel as hard as we could in an effort to miss the dock, but not a chance. We hit the telephone pole pilings, snapping them like pretzels one after another until Gratitude finally got her forward gear activated. Then, with a mighty surge, she leaped toward the Puget Sound, pulling away from the now crumbling dock.

Jamie and I looked at each other, sick to our stomachs and pale white. In panic, we agreed. If the captain did this destructive maneuver on the simple chore of backing out, what on earth was he going to do on the difficult job of coming back in? What were we going to tell Don?

As we pulled out into the harbor, we heard shouting. Everyone on the dock was yelling, "That ship hit that pier!"—as if it wasn't obvious enough.

This pier was a fuel dock over the Puget Sound, which made a bad situation even more serious. The fireboat Chief of Seattle, with all its fire fighting gear came racing to the scene. Police cars, fire trucks and Coast Guard boats emerged at Pier 70, where we had to return.

The rest of this sea trial proved uneventful and, thankfully, the ship came in for a surprisingly soft landing. The lines went out, the ship was tied fast and properly, and the crew immediately stretched the gangway across to the dock. Jamie and I reluctantly crossed the gangway to meet our accusers. We walked back along the pier to inspect the damage to the rear of the ship. Our swift-footed supreme court judge-rear admiral "captain" approached Jamie and me with a swagger. "Oh well, Sondra, these things happen. How's our insurance?"

"What insurance?" I asked, shaking my head.

He leaned in close to Jamie and whispered, "Plead the fifth, son," then walked off leaving us to face the music.

But facing the police, the fireboats, the fire trucks and the Coast Guard wasn't our greatest fear. We had a greater milestone to get by that evening. It was Don. Somehow we'd have to explain this disaster to him.

Don:

That day I had been inspecting a ship for a possible third acquisition. I returned to hear the wonderful news of how well Gratitude ran—right through the pier—and how really strong she was, how I should be proud of her. She only had one little dent. As I sat listening to my wife reconstruct the debacle, Jamie nodded his head profusely in agreement. I thought, *Most men's wives tell them, "Honey, I put this little bitty dent in the family car." But my wife plows down half of the Seattle waterfront with a ship!*

Needless to say, the Coast Guard was hot on my tail. They demanded an immediate inquiry and a full investigation of the incident.

Of course, we didn't have a dime to pay for that dock and all the damage. The next day down at the fuel dock, while doing a little investigating, I spoke with an oil company employee standing by the main gate. "It's a real shame that a ship rammed into your dock."

He replied, "Yeah. They did a good job of tearing her up. But it really doesn't matter. It hasn't been announced yet but just last week the city condemned this dock. There's nothing wrong with the dock, you see, but they had to condemn it to build something else here."

"Do you mean that as it sits right now, this is just an old condemned dock not in service?"

"That's right," he said. "We just haven't taken down the business signs yet."

"Nice talking to you. Have a good day," I smiled and left.

I prepared my defense and went to the Coast Guard hearing.

All the brass was there. The inquiry began. The Coast Guard investigation officer was nice, knowing quite well they had us over a big barrel. "You understand, Mr. Tipton, that we don't wish you and your charity any hardship, but you caused a great deal of damage. There are fines to consider; I'm sure there will be lawsuits, and we may have to impound your ship Gratitude. You may possibly have to forfeit your ship Spirit as well."

I was quite polite myself. After explaining about the type of charity we represented, I mentioned that I was very happy that the Union Oil company had the Coast Guard for their spokesman on legal affairs.

Sounding quite assured (with an official note to my voice), I said, "Let me address you directly. Through extensive investigations by our staff, it has come to our attention that this old dilapidated Pier 71 has been condemned by the City of Seattle and slated for destruction.

"With no lights, 'condemned' signs or warnings of any kind, our innocent ship backed out of Pier 70 on its harmless journey into the Puget Sound when this menace to navigation, this old condemned pier directly in our right of way, struck our ship, causing damage and great emotional stress.

"But we want to assure you that we are quality people and don't want to bring any hardship on you, the city or the fuel company. We are the type of people that would never consider bringing lawsuits and liability damages against the fuel company, the harbor department, the City of Seattle, or the negligent Coast Guard. After all, it is your responsibility to post hazardous warnings. We'll take the damage to our ship in stride and remain friends. We will stand responsible for the damages caused to our vessel, if you four will take financial responsibility for your damages."

The review board stared at me and then broke out into smiles. They knew I had a strong case, as ridiculous as it was. The investigator said, "Touché, Mr. Tipton. Touché." We adjourned the meeting and never heard another word about the pier from the Coast Guard, the Police Department, the Fire Department, the City of Seattle or the fuel company.

Later, we moved the ship uneventfully through the locks into Lake Union. We tied up to a beautiful pier, worked on the ship and readied it to receive cargo for its first voyage.

A few months had passed when my old friend Paul Watson came to visit us. Paul was one of the originators of Greenpeace and had since founded the Sea Shepherd Conservation Society— a marine mammal protection agency which takes aggressive action against illegal whaling, sealing and fishing operations.

A most extreme conservation group, their activities have included the sinking of several notorious ships which had been used for hunting whales in violation of marine mammal protection treaties. People often called Paul and his men "environmental guerrillas." Japanese fishermen often became targets of Sea Shepherd's campaigns because of their illegal whaling activities.

Before turning our lives over to Jesus, Sondra and I worked on behalf of the Sea Shepherd, and we still have particularly strong feelings for the creations of God, especially His animals. Although we believe that Jesus may be coming soon and are expending all of our time to save God's children, we are also aware of our stewardship responsibility for all His creations who have no voice.

On his way through Seattle to visit us (as he often did), Paul happened to drive past Gratitude. When he arrived at the Spirit, he said, "Don, I want you to drive back over to the lake with me. While driving by on the freeway, I saw a ship on Lake Union at a distance . I've never seen a ship so beautiful. She looks powerful and fast, more like a sports fishing yacht than a commercial ship. Looks to be about 200 feet in length. She has a beautiful paint job of three or four shades of blue. Come back over and help me find it. I've got to know more about this ship. It's just what I'm looking for."

"I know this ship, Paul," I said to him. "She's everything you say and more, but she's not for sale."

Surprised, Paul asked, "How do you know this?"

"Because the vessel belongs to us, Paul," I said.

He couldn't believe it. "Not this one. It's not an old cargo ship. It's the most beautiful ship on the water."

I explained to him how we had acquired the ship. He was utterly amazed.

Paul then told us, "I'm here in town to attend an auction of a large tuna vessel super-seiner. I heard it's well maintained and an extremely powerful ship, but I'm afraid it's going to sell for a lot of money." Paul went on by himself to the auction, and at auction time no one else appeared to bid on the ship. By the time the hammer was dropped on the auction, Paul had bought the ship for a minimum bid.

We went over to look at his prize catch—a beautiful ship called the Bold Venture. Walking through the vessel, we noticed that it was very unlike the Japanese-built Gratitude. The head room was high enough for us, and the bunks were big enough for our North American-sized crews to turn over in.

On Gratitude, although the rooms and the bunks were meticulous and the ship was beautifully appointed, but the sleeping berths still looked like they belonged in a doll house. Also, if you were 5'7" or taller, you bumped your head along the ceiling as you walked.

All of the instruments and instructions on the Bold Venture were in English. The start, the stop, the forward, the reverse— we could read everything. That was an advantage over Gratitude.

After we toured the ship, Paul looked at me and said, "Don, why don't we trade? This ship has room for more cargo and it has big booms that will handle all the gear, cargo slings and nets. You can even load cars, buses and trucks on deck."

I thought, *It's time to do some more horse trading.*

His ship was more valuable than ours but I wanted to try an unbelievable trade anyway. "Paul, you know that I owe five payments of $10,000 and a balloon payment of $50,000, so I'll tell you what I'll do. I'll trade my ship for your ship if you make my first two payments."

"Hmmm," he said, with his eyes on mine. "I'll speak to the board of directors and get back to you shortly." At that we parted company.

The next day, Paul drove up. He strolled up in his usual manner showing himself to be a soft, quiet, humble human being with kind mannerisms. "Don, I've spoken to the board," he sighed, "and we don't like your deal."

Not too surprised I replied "Oh, I didn't think you would."

"We have an alternate proposal," Paul offered.

"Okay, let's hear it."

"This is the way it'll go," he outlined. "We'll take your ship and you take our ship—straight across. Then we'll make *all* your payments."

I stared at Paul, realizing he was offering to make a large contribution to our organization. He held out his hand and said "Is it a deal?"

I took his hand and said, "I think we can live with that deal, Paul. No problem."

Glory to God, we had acquired another ship, bigger, better and more useful. And we had yet to spend hardly a dime!

We switched the name Gratitude to our new ship and Paul gave the name "Divine Wind" to the ship that had been Gratitude. A few weeks later, Divine Wind sailed from Puget Sound, its crew looking for illegal gill netters and men who would kill whales and their calves in violation of international treaties. Our crew waved a warm good-bye from the shore.

We began to prepare the new Gratitude for a mission to the Philippines. We had no funds, no crew, no cargo and no fuel, but we set a date of August 15 for our sail date to the Philippines.

Gratitude needed to be dry-docked in a shipyard, which is a very expensive undertaking. We estimated the hull work to be done at over $20,000.

We called different shipyards, asking if they would consider helping us for free. A man at a shipyard in Bellingham, Washington, listened to our story. He said he had a small plane

Gratitude

The First Gratitude

and would fly to where the Gratitude was moored on Lake Union to have a look. When he arrived, we toured him through the vessel and gave him as much information as we had on the condition of the ship's hull. She was in good shape and would only need routine service, chipping and painting. We sat down on the stairwell together and he thought things over for a moment. Then he said his company would do the job—no charge!

We took the ship in for dry dock where she was pampered like a baby for ten days—free of charge.

As we sailed Gratitude back from Bellingham to Seattle, we were under the command of a foreign-licensed captain. Jamie and I were aboard, as well as some crew members and guests who came along for the ride. Sondra and a few other crew members were ashore to meet us at Pier 70. The owners there had given us permission again to dock at no charge.

All went well until we started the approach. The captain had a beautiful heart and good credentials but hadn't been in command of a ship for nearly thirty years. He also had a heavy foreign accent and sometimes we misunderstood what he would say. But I was at peace because also on board as a passenger was Captain George Folden, a man licensed to sail any ship, in any ocean around the world—and he had done it.

George was not in command of Gratitude that day and had nothing to do with the operations of the ship but it was still a comfort to have him there. Also, inside the wheelhouse was another precious and experienced friend named John, who had graciously agreed to take the helm.

The foreign Captain decided to aim Gratitude's bow at Pier 69, a nice dock with a large warehouse. His intention, apparently, was to pull up to Pier 69 and back into the space at Pier 70. That was fine, but I realized as we approached that we needed to slow down.

Gratitude weighed almost a thousand tons. A vessel of that size takes a long time to slow or to reverse engines. John was at the throttle and he soon realized we were in trouble, but because it is opposed to all standards of maritime ethics to seize command from the captain, John was virtually helpless to do anything about it.

The captain had either grossly miscalculated the speed, the ability of the ship to switch gears, the distance, or perhaps we had a language barrier. Regardless of the reason, the situation was serious. I ran up to the bridge.

"Astern, Captain?" I heard John suggest, anxiously.

"No," the Captain replied, "ahead."

I could see George Folden pacing up and down, up and down, with his hands behind his back, working his fingers in his hands. He was becoming extremely nervous. We were headed into the dock fast, much, much too fast.

As George paced, John looked at me desperately, his eyes in a panic, as if to say, "What do I do? What do I do?"

Suddenly, George rushed forward, grabbed the rail in front of him with white knuckles and shouted to the women who were standing on the bow enjoying the cruise, without a hint that we were in trouble. He shouted in a commanding voice, "You women get off the bow now. CLEAR THE BOW NOW! I said now—do as I say!"

John grabbed the reverse throttle and looked back at me, then asked the captain again, "Reverse, Captain? Astern? Astern?"

"Ahead," said the captain. It was then that we realized the captain must have reverse and forward confused. He was saying forward when he meant to say astern.

The language barrier had gotten us into deep trouble. I jumped in with a loud voice and yelled to John, "Astern! Astern! Now! Right now!" John jammed the throttle back but there was no reaction. Captain George was still pacing. I knew we were in great danger.

As the ship headed at collision speed toward Pier 69, there was nothing that could be done. Her throttle was full astern and the engines were screaming, but we still had no reaction from the vessel. Looking to the forward of the ship I could see that we were steaming straight for a collision into the pier. I ran toward the bow, thinking *I've gotta see this.* Then I thought, *No, I don't want to see this,* and I headed toward the stern. *No, there will be an inquiry. I've got to see this,* and I headed forward again. Our speed hardly decreased. It was all too obvious now we were going to ram the pier.

By this time the shore crew thought we'd gone crazy. It appeared as if we were simply taking a full-on run at the pier and all its buildings. They were certain we were going to hit. It was obvious that a ship the size of Gratitude could not stop, slow down or reverse engines in time to avoid a collision with the dock.

The big question was, "How bad will the collision be?" Would the ship go through the dock and warehouse, winding up on the waterfront street or would she be destroyed—or both? Sondra yelled to the women and children who still stood along Gratitude's upper rail, "Move back. Move back from the rail!" but she could not be heard above Gratitude's powerful main engine. Our crewman Butch was running up and down the dock screaming, "We bought it! We bought it!"

People shrieked from the dock, "Look! That ship is going to crash into that building! It's gonna crash!" Butch continued to run up and down the dock shouting, "We bought it, we bought it!" Then I heard George say from behind me, "We're going to ram her." I saw him run forward to the port side bridge wing, look over the side to evaluate the imminent collision as the dock quickly disappeared beneath the bow of the ship. He threw his arms over his head and yelled "Oh, (word deleted)! We're going to ram her, we're going to ram her!" I heard George holler one last "Oh, (word deleted)! We're going to ram her!" and I yelled, "No, in the name of Jesus. Stop in the name of Jesus!"

At that moment, a miracle happened. Gratitude stopped— not suddenly, although it was all at once, but without any kind of jerk that a sudden stop from a hard run would create. The ship just simply stopped dead in the water and gently bobbed up and down, as if in some kind of bubble, not even jarring the women and children who still stood at the rail on deck.

There was a dead silence, not even the sound of a distant sea gull could be heard. Even the roar of our powerful engines in reverse seemed to be silent. I looked forward to see the ship looming over Pier 69. I looked at Sondra, who was holding up her hands to indicate that the bow of the ship, at the level where it would have collided with the dock, was only **one foot** from impact.

Captain George grabbed my shoulders with both hands, visibly shocked. He stood with his face in my face and said, "Don, do you realize what just happened?" He continued to hold me with both hands as he repeated, "All my life I've wondered about miracles. I've never seen one but now I have and now I know. This was a real miracle." We were both stunned—and relieved beyond description.

After a few moments, we slowly backed the ship away from the dock. The captain completed the maneuver with complete control. No one present that day would ever be the same. There was no natural way to explain what had happened.

We had witnessed an absolute, physical miracle of God—a miracle that had saved us from certain financial ruin. Not one of us really understood what had happened as well as did Captain George, who knew God had saved us and our ship. He was a man who had sailed the seas for many years, in calm and stormy weather, and had docked in more countries and more ports than he could remember. He had (almost) seen it all.

You may be interested to know that with each dock and city that we threatened, we **did** get a little better at handling the ships.

8

A TUG IN THE RIGHT DIRECTION

I had been thinking over our eventual need for huge amounts of cargo and had it on my mind to acquire a tugboat. Whether it was the Lord inspiring me or my own simple thoughts, I'm not sure. My plan was to run a barge and tug up the Sacramento River. We could make friends with the local farmers and load the barge with every good thing they had surplus. Maybe we could even bring it out into the harbor and transfer the cargo to our ships. This seemed like smart thinking to me. *This must be what the Lord has in mind.* I checked our bank account to make absolutely sure it was as empty as it usually was. It was. I then started to work toward acquiring a tug, even going so far as to attend tugboat auctions.

But, I soon found out that tugboat owners are very proud of their boats and they want a lot of money for them. They didn't take too kindly to the suggestion of giving them away.

Then I heard through the grapevine about a tugboat, a big one. It was about 140 feet of sheer power, one of the larger tugs on the Pacific Coast, and was currently moored on the Petaluma River. According to the description, the tug had four stories above the water and one below, and all the winches and power we would ever need. It was a bargain, a fire sale. The owner was only asking a half a million dollars. This seemed like a proper tugboat for us so we made an appointment with the owner, a man named Don Hughes.

Hughes was large with bright red hair and a nautical type

beard, ruggedly handsome, like one of the old seaman they paint in pictures. His voice sounded like soft thunder, and he had even once owned a bar on the San Francisco waterfront.

Jamie and I made our way to Northern California where Mr. Hughes was kind enough to pick us up from the airport. He drove us to a ranch in Petaluma where the tug was moored along the banks of the Petaluma River. Parking his big Mercedes in the mud, Mr. Hughes got out and led us sloshing through the mire, over the top of the levy bank toward the river.

There she sat, this marvelous old tug, tied to a giant oak tree. Mr. Hughes toured us all through the beautiful vessel, giving a four-hour presentation, leaving nothing out.

Now we were together in the galley. "Would you care to see anything else?" he asked in his deep, strong voice.

"No, I think you've adequately shown me everything I need to see," I replied.

Looking down at me, his broad shoulders came square to mine. The time for the deal had come. "You've seen my boat. How do you like her?"

"Oh, I like her. She's certainly a fine boat—everything you say she is."

"You've heard the price. How do you like that?"

"Oh, I think it's a fine price at half a million, below market I'm sure, for such a dignified ship."

"Well, I guess you'll take her then."

"Yes, sir, I certainly want to take her..."

"Good. Then it's done," he said with a slight smile.

"But there's one small problem," I said. "I don't have a dime."

"What?" he boomed out as he leaned over and stared deep into my eyes.

There was silence. We stared at each other for a long time; no one blinked. I then said, "Mr. Hughes, God has need of your tugboat."

There was another deep stare. Mr. Hughes' thundering voice

softened as he replied, "Well, Sonny, if God has need of my tugboat, I wouldn't be caught dead with it," and he meant that literally. (He proved to be a man of his word by turning over the title papers to the tug—free and clear.) There we were, the proud new owners of a tugboat, papers in hand, not a dime against her!

To celebrate, we decided to go to town and buy some bread, bologna and juice, come back and have lunch aboard the tug.

"Isn't it strange?" I said to Jamie. "Here's this giant tugboat tied to a tree on the bank of the Petaluma with no other boats around."

When we came back a little later to the tugboat, a gentleman farmer named Neill Smith was waiting for us.

Smith was the man who owned the tree that the tugboat was tied off to, along with hundreds of acres of one of the most beautiful farms in Petaluma, complete with a giant old farmhouse. He was a likable man who seemed kind and caring, a handsome, educated ivy league type with an esoteric way of thinking, while maintaining an upper crust posture. It was a charming combination, and we hit it off from the start.

"You're the new owner?" he asked. "I was wondering how soon you'll be moving the tug."

"I guess I'll move it downtown," I said, "as soon as I can arrange for a free dock."

He smiled and said, "It came here from downtown. You wouldn't think so, but there's a shortage of pier space for a ship your size, tugboats and barges and such."

"Oh," I said. "I wasn't aware of a shortage of dock space."

"Yes, you see, nine other tugboats have applied for your same tree."

"Please, Mr. Smith, would you join us for some bologna sandwiches in the galley and we can discuss my dilemma."

Mr. Smith explained to us that he was an architect from San Francisco and had established a firm that built many of San Francisco's recognizable structures. One day, he said, he took a

Tugboat Reverence (tied to a tree)

look at the structures he had created and decided to take up farming. Tired of being part of the whole overdevelopment "problem", he decided instead, he said, to be part of the "answer." Now he owned and operated this big, beautiful farm, a place where fat old cows wandered wherever they wanted. Jamie and I were immediately impressed with him.

Smith asked us to explain about the mission we were on, so I told him what we wanted to do with this old tugboat and our ship in Seattle. He said, "I'll go to Seattle with you and take a look at all this." And he did.

Neill flew up to Seattle and spent several days with us aboard Spirit. We became fast friends. He decided that the tugboat would be his guest, no charge. All was free. Our new good friend Mr. Smith was dying of cancer at this time but neither of us knew it. He has since died. Now he himself is being hosted forever beside a riverside by our Father in heaven. I'm sure he and Jesus have had talks about the good old tugboat that was tied off to a tree.

Later, as a reminder of the reverence we felt toward God at giving us this magnificent tugboat, we decided to call her just that—"Reverence."

Finances were at an all time low. We had three ships and many crew members to support. What small funds we had were stretched thin, so we were praying for a way to meet our obligations. Then an interesting thing happened.

The "Yardarm Knot", a sister ship to the Spirit, arrived at the pier next to us. She was badly in need of a paint job. We had just completed painting the hull on Spirit. It had taken the crew a month of steady work to complete the job. The paint had been donated. (We had received 6,000 gallons, which was much more than we would need for the next couple of years.) The owners of the Yardarm offered to pay us $6,500 to paint their vessel if we would use some of our donated paint. This offer sounded good since we had a $1,300 dockage bill to pay on Gratitude. However, up to this point, we hadn't worked for money to fund the ministry and we weren't sure how the crew would react. Still, we needed money, but we had no solicitation of funds and no way to raise them. We had prayed for a provision and felt it was important not to overlook this opportunity.

After we thought it over, we decided that we couldn't put Jesus in a box. Just because we hadn't done work for money before was no reason to dismiss this provision.

We asked the crew for their participation. When I told them of the opportunity, some yelled, "No." Many frowned.

I recognized that I'd run into a religious bone of contention. I asked, "Can we have a show of hands for those who will join in painting?" The hands shot up and most were more than willing to help. Some still maintained that we were "selling out." They hadn't come to work outside this ministry, they said. But most of us agreed that for this particular time, the opportunity presented itself, and if we used the money to pay the bills for the ship, we were still working for God.

The ship we were to paint was tied up on the front of the pier, facing Puget Sound. Our men were so energetic that they began to paint the Yardarm in record time. Amazingly, what had taken us a month to do on the Spirit, we were completing now in only forty-eight hours. The ship looked beautiful! The two vessels looked like twins sitting side by side.

The crew of the Yardarm leaned over their rail, watching our guys work. The Spirit crew talked with them, inviting several to our Sunday morning church service, but the men seemed disinterested or noncommittal about attending.

Wedged between the dock and the Yardarm Knot were two giant rubber tires that kept the huge ship from scraping up against the dock. The breeze was on the outside, pushing the ship tightly against the pier. One of the men from the Yardarm hollered down to one of our men, "I'd like to see how you're going to paint behind those tires, my friend."

"Don't worry, by the time we get there, God will do something," our man said.

The Yardarm crew shook their heads and chuckled,

convinced they were talking to some religious nuts. "If God does something when you get to that tire, I'll be at your church on Sunday," one said.

The ferry boats that run the Puget Sound from island to shore are large and sail very fast. The regularly running ferry boats pass by every few hours. Later that day, a tug pulling a loaded barge came into Puget Sound and approached the Seattle waterfront. The ferry had to divert around the tug and barge. It was delayed because of this. Trying to make up time, it raced down the waterfront, closer than we've ever seen a ferry boat come before. As he powered by us, the ferry created a large wave that rocked both ships. They pulled back against their ropes and rocked back to the docks. Amazingly, this wave action flipped both tires up beside the Yardarm where they stayed, lodged lengthwise between the boat and the dock, exposing the area that needed to be painted.

The crew of both ships witnessed this unusual event. Our crew couldn't believe it anymore than the men from the Yardarm could. Never before had this happened in the years we'd been there at these docks and never did we see it happen again. But this one special time, at just the right moment, God had played a trick on our new friends.

We worked quickly to paint the right places. As the next ferry boat came in, going in the opposite direction and doing the same fast diversion, the ship pulled back from the dock, stretched the lines out and our men shoved the tires back into place against the hull. As the boat pushed back to the dock and cushioned itself against the tires, our crew glanced up at the Yardarm men, "That's how it's done," they said.

We had a great laugh about the incident and Sunday morning several of the crew members of the Yardarm came to the church service, keeping their end of the bargain. What a story we had to tell!

When we received the $6,500 payment, Jamie felt the Lord wanted us to offer each crew member $50. As we called everyone together to distribute the pay, it is interesting to note that not one man or woman, even those who felt it was "wrong" to take the job, felt it was "wrong" to take the money.

We paid our bills, the money ran out and, once again, we had no funds to pay the new obligations. There were no more ships to paint and Gratitude was running up bills fast as she prepared to sail. We were offered a job to reroof a house, tile the bathroom and kitchen, replace the carpet, repaint and clean up for $2,500.

This time there were no religious disputes about it. All were in agreement, happy to do the work, and we finished the job quickly. Never again has the Lord asked us to work outside of our operation. I'm still not certain why He did then, but it's all okay with me.

9

THIRTY-DAY MIRACLE

One day in the late spring, Sondra was speaking on the phone with a minister from Nigeria who asked why we weren't ready to run missions with the Spirit ship. She told him that, among other things, we still needed hundreds of thousands of dollars' worth of engine parts.

The minister finished his conversation with Sondra and handed the phone to another party, then a few minutes later asked to speak to her again. He said that the Lord had just told him that we would have all the engine parts we needed **within four weeks.** She thanked him but didn't take this word of encouragement too seriously because over the past few years we had heard many supposedly prophetic words that had not come true. However, this time would prove to be different.

A couple of days later, after some appointments on shore Sondra returned to the ship. Walking through the passageways and into the galley, she felt an unexplainable excitement in the air. It was as if something had happened, something good.

When she reached the mess hall, she found me and said, "I feel like something has happened. I can feel it in the air." With a huge smile, I blurted out, "Something certainly has!" I began to tell her that during that morning while she was gone, to my great surprise, a man walked on board—a man whose name I'd heard but who I didn't know. This man was John Hauff.

John was about my age, but tall and slim, and had the kindest eyes I'd ever seen.

We sat down over a cup of coffee in the mess hall, and he opened with, "I'm part owner of the Rose Knot, an exact sister ship to this one. It was a spy ship used by the government to track the Gemini capsule in the NASA space program. Rose Knot is fully equipped with every part imaginable and then some.

"For business reasons of our own, my partner and I are selling the ship. I know you're missing a lot of parts from your wheelhouse all the way to the engine room, and I'm aware of how hard these parts are to come by. The parts you need will make no difference to us or the buyer. The ship is a treasure house for you, but the problem is we're closing the deal very soon, so you **only have four weeks** to get the parts off Rose Knot."

Sadly I said, "I'm sorry, as bad as we need these parts, we have no money. I know you're talking about hundreds of thousands of dollars worth of parts but we have less than $100 in our safe."

John replied, "Oh, no, you don't understand; we want to **give** them to you. But you'll have to come and get them right away."

The next morning, the crew and I drove to the Rose Knot in Tacoma. We knew the ship was anchored about a mile or so out and had no power, so we brought a 12-foot aluminum skiff, some lamps, candles and flashlights, and all the tools we could find. What parts weren't loose, we would unbolt. John Hauff looked at the eighteen of us standing there with our skiff, blankets and pillows, food and sandwich coolers, jars of water and jugs of milk. He fought back a laugh and said, "What are you going to do with that little bitty aluminum skiff, with no motor?"

"This is all we have that floats," I replied.

John shook his head and said, "Don't go anywhere; I'll be back."

A few minutes later, we heard the roar of a loud engine and saw the stack on a big tugboat blowing black. John tooted the horn and poked his head out from the bridge, waving us over. We ran down the beach toward the tug with everything we could carry, tripping over our gear, excited to have a ride out on a big, safe tugboat.

We pulled up beside the Rose Knot on John's tug, climbed aboard and shifted all our gear to the deck. Grabbing our candles and flashlights, we entered into the bowels of this giant ship.

We must have seemed like kids in a candy store. It was a vast treasure house, dark and cold like King Tut's tomb but laden with every good thing that it would take to put Spirit to sea for years to come.

To our amazement, we saw a huge cache of parts with our vessel's name and labels on them. Our missing parts were found! John explained that some years ago the previous owner of the Spirit had sold the parts to the previous owners of the Rose Knot. It was a double blessing, Rose Knot's equipment and Spirit's, ours for the taking. Before us was a veritable fortune in spare parts. With a lit candle in one hand and a wrench in the other, we began to dismantle the things we needed.

John stood back and watched, then wandered through the dark ship shaking his head. "This will never do." John took a fuel hose and threw it over the side of the ship, down onto the decks of his tugboat. He then stuck the hose deep into his own fuel tanks, connected the other end to the giant locomotive generators aboard the Rose Knot, opened the ship's valves and started the motors. All of a sudden, the engines roared and the ship lit up like a Christmas tree. We extinguished our candles. Now we could use both hands to work and boy, did we make use of them!

With us during that special time was my beloved friend, Cecil Sinclair, who had come to be like my own father. Cecil, a (mostly) American Indian (and he looked the part), had met and joined us in the early days of Spirit and had stood by me in every hard time. It's a boy's childhood dream to have someone who watches your backside, a kind of rear guard, looking out for your best interests. Well, Cecil was mine and was until (as this book went to press) God called him home.

Here was every piece of equipment we had been praying for, including diesel injectors for our big main engine. The injectors had been one of our highest priorities and Cecil, especially, had been seeking the Lord for them. Now he sat straddled atop the engines, saying, "Nobody touch these injectors; these are mine!" He then began to gather them up, take them ashore and load these big, heavy parts into the trunk of his Ford LTD, promptly breaking the rear springs of the car. But Cecil didn't care. He knew these parts were a miracle from God, and he was determined to drive them to the Spirit himself.

Next, we took out two-ton main engine pistons and heavy sleeve liners, dragging them down the hallways to a place they could be lifted off the ship. John Hauff continued to shake his head. "If you try to put that 2,000 pound piston in your 12 foot skiff, they'll both be at the bottom of the sea."

"We don't know what we'll do, but we'll think of something. God must have an answer," we replied. John pumped some fuel into a tank so we could continue to operate, then sailed off in his tugboat. A few hours later, he and the tug came back, only this time, he was pushing a great big barge with a crane in the middle. He began to operate the crane, taking everything we gathered and placing it into his barge.

Over the next couple of weeks, our men worked marathon hours, and each day John Hauff made trips with his barge from the ship to the shore, loaded with parts. He borrowed trucks from a friend and helped us run loads to the Spirit. Soon, the dock alongside Spirit and her main deck were piled high with every sort of spare part and piece of equipment we could imagine, so much so, you could hardly walk on the deck or the dock, and still the truck loads continued to arrive.

We brought home over a million dollars worth of parts and equipment from the Rose Knot that month, including most of the wheelhouse gear, engine room parts and needed spares. Amazingly, we were finished and out in four weeks, just as the Nigerian minister had prophesied!

Another coincidence, eh? Don't you believe it!

10

TEXAS LOOSEY'S

It was time for Gratitude to make her maiden mercy voyage. We planned to run down the West Coast to gather up supplies and then to turn her bow toward the Philippine Islands. It was a brave plan and was going to take some faith since we only had $12 in the bank and hardly enough fuel to get out of Puget Sound.

We had agreed that for now we wouldn't ask anyone for money. We had a challenge. Before we could sail, we had to come up with money for oil pollution insurance, which is required by Coast Guard regulations. We also needed to move Spirit from Pier 66 to Pier 91 before Sondra, Jamie and I could leave town with Gratitude. Finally, it was time to consider vessel registration for the Gratitude.

We wanted to register her as a yacht because she was a private vessel with volunteer crew members who neither paid for passage nor were paid as crew. We intended only to carry gifts as donations to the poor. We would do absolutely no commercial service. In order to register as an American yacht, we would have fallen under regulations that would have been difficult for this ship to comply with since Gratitude was originally constructed as a fishing vessel. So, we decided that our best registry would be as foreign yacht.

About this time, a wonderful friend named Peter Chignell—who ran a prison ministry on the South Pacific Island of Tonga and was in the U.S. on a speaking tour—came to stay with us on the ship. Peter was an eloquent gentlemen from New Zealand who had worked for the New Zealand school board as superintendent for Tonga's educational system. Late in his career, he decided to take an early retirement, give up all of his earthly belongings and move into the horrendous Tonga prison to live and work as their chaplain. Like the inmates, he slept on the floor with the rats and the bugs. He spent his days ministering to the prisoners, working to improve their living conditions and giving Bible studies inside the prison and at the palace. Peter was thrilled to have the privilege of leading two men—the nation's prime minister and Tonga's most notorious murderer—hand in hand—in a prayer of commitment to Jesus.

We had fallen in love with this man and with the great measure of Christ's love that we found in him.

When we discussed our registration situation with Peter, he asked us to consider registering Gratitude in Tonga. He said he would make all the arrangements with the Tongan government. We agreed and he began to work with the palace on our behalf.

Although they were pleased to receive our ship's registry, the prince who was in charge of maritime affairs told us that they had not yet designed official "documentation" for yachts, as Tongan yachts required no documentation.

So, by the time we were ready to sail, we still had no document in hand. The Coast Guard informed us that it was not possible to leave port without proper papers and, as far as we knew, leaving port without an official document had never been legally done. But, we did have a telegram which said that the Tongan government welcomed the vessel Gratitude as a Tongan yacht, "in principle", although they had no official (or even unofficial) paperwork for now. The trick would be to convince the U.S. Coast Guard that it would be okay to let us sail internationally with only a telegram from the King of Tonga as a document.

When next we met with the Coast Guard, we explained to the local officials that Tonga had issued a telegram that, as far as they were concerned, allowed us to sail. Meanwhile, a not-so-friendly Coast Guard official who had caused us problems in the past, sent a telegram to the King of the Kingdom of Tonga, without informing us. It read, something like, "The United States Coast Guard is allowing Tonga's yacht Gratitude to sail from Puget Sound, but it will not be welcome back in U.S. waters." This telegram had far-reaching effects since, at about that same time, negotiations were in process to establish a U.S. naval base and air strip in this island nation. Also, Tonga had precious fishing grounds scattered throughout its many waters that were of great interest to our American fishing fleets.

We heard that when the King of Tonga received the telegram and read that his only official yacht was no longer welcome in America and that this determination had been made through a captain in the Coast Guard, with no notice from the State Department or from our President, he was infuriated. It was unheard of that such an official act of the United States government had taken place without negotiations or proper protocol. He considered it an insult to him and all his people.

I received a phone call from a very alarmed Peter Chignell. He said that the King was furious that the United States would treat him with such utter disregard and that he was preparing a letter of retaliation to the President, demanding the removal of all American flag vessels from Tongan territory and their 200-mile fishing limit. Furthermore, no American ship would be welcome in Tongan waters.

The U.S. State Department was extremely alarmed and obviously upset that a local Coast Guard captain would take it upon himself to dictate foreign policy to another sovereign country. This was a great mistake. So, now it seemed we had become a political "hot potato" to the Coast Guard and they began to treat us carefully. They issued us our safety inspection certificates and lifted the port hold off the ship. Even though, our only document was still just a telegram, we now had full unprecedented Coast Guard approval!

As the Coast Guard officers were leaving the ship from their inspection, all paperwork complete, a lieutenant said, "Oh, by the way, have you checked things out with Customs?" I answered, "We're not leaving the United States, we're only going down the coast now, so we thought we'd check with Customs before going out of San Diego."

"Oh, of course," he replied. "Everything is okay with us for you to sail, but as a small favor to me, would you mind just calling Customs and telling them that you're leaving? The Coast Guard comes under the authority of Customs and that would be good procedure." I said I would. Jamie and I talked about how polite the Coast Guard had become. We were pleased at how different their attitude was now from the hostile posture they had adopted for the past several months.

We gave Customs a call as we said we would. As I explained our reason for calling, the Customs official on the other end of the phone seemed quite familiar with our ship's situation. "Why are you calling me?" she said. "We've settled this with the Coast Guard. They were told that under no circumstances would you be allowed to leave port. No ship enters and leaves American waters without proper documentation. It isn't done. It hasn't been done since the establishment of our maritime laws, and it won't be done now."

We told the official about our Coast Guard inspections and what they had said to us. "I don't know what games are being played," she replied. "They've been speaking to us on this matter for several days. They know our position well. I can tell you it won't do any good, but I'll call Washington, D.C. It's late in the day there so I'll have to hang up and call them right now."

A few minutes later, the phone rang. It was the official from Customs. She was quite astonished and said, bewildered, "I don't know who you know in Washington but they told me to release you and accommodate you however we can—hands off.

"So," she continued, "as crazy as it sounds, this is the way it's got to happen. Customs is viewing you as an American fishing boat and the Coast Guard sees you as a Tongan yacht. You don't have paperwork for either one but, we've been told not to stand in your way. So, if you see what appears to be a Customs officer, run up the American flag and consider yourself a U.S. fishing boat. If you have any problems, they can call me. But, if you see the Coast Guard, get out your Tongan flag and run it up. If you run into problems, refer them back here to the Seattle Coast Guard. I haven't heard of anything like this in my whole career and neither has anyone else in this whole office, so Godspeed."

We loaded up supplies aboard Gratitude and planned our trip: stops in San Francisco, Sacramento, Los Angeles and San Diego, picking up supplies for the Philippines.

Then we shifted Gratitude from Pier 70 to Pier 66 and promptly experienced a long series of mishaps. Our engine crew had run the generator out of fuel and it died just as we were about to back out. As we were casting off, the main engine shut down because our bright, but inexperienced, engineer had borrowed a valve, moving it from one spot to another, then forgetting to move it back. The lines tangled and the bow of the ship aimed straight for Pier 70! We got the engine started just in the nick of time and sailed from Pier 70.

As we arrived at Pier 66, there was some trouble with the lines and the stern swung out toward the Edgewater Hotel. Somehow, we managed to dock her without further embarrassing incident.

Agnes Numer's group, Somerhaven Ranch, had a long standing relationship with a Los Angeles area Church of the Nazarene minister who had given them some problems. We had decided to give him a wide berth because each time Somerhaven dealt with him, it seemed to us that it created a worse situation than the time before. But Somerhaven, in their mercy, continued to help him and minister to him whenever they could. They told him of our small ship Gratitude sailing to the Philippines. He was given our phone number and, after some special arrangements of his own, he decided he'd do us a great big favor.

He called me on the phone and told me that my problems

were over. He had made arrangements with a woman from a Philippine family—very close friends of his who were extremely rich—to pay for all of our expenses to the Philippines. Whatever I needed, I just had to name it.

So I asked who this rich lady was who claimed to be willing to spend any amount of money. "Oh," he said, "she's well connected in high places in the Philippines."

I said, "How high and how political and who are you talking about?" That's when he announced that his friend was the niece of the deposed dictator of the Philippines, Ferdinand Marcos!

"Listen," I said, my voice very direct, "I want you to hear me very clearly. You do not have my permission to talk to anybody regarding my ships. You never have had and you never will have. I have never spoken to anybody in the Marcos regime." (Ferdinand Marcos, only a few weeks before, had been accused of trying to ship arms into the Philippines in a failed attempt to overthrow the present government.) "I'm going to hang up the phone now. Please don't ever call me again regarding anything to do with the Philippines or the Marcos'." I hung up, naively thinking that I had put a decisive end to it.

I knew that for us to carry anything aboard Gratitude originating from the Marcos family was undoubtedly a political ploy and sure death to our mission. If word of a possible relationship between us and the Marcos' leaked out to the Philippine government, our ship would be turned away with all the gifts that were to go to the children and the poor.

Two days later at nine o'clock in the evening, Sondra took a call at the Spirit office. It was from a reporter in Hawaii who told her he had received on the wire, a story that representatives of the Marcos family was claiming over national radio that they were sending relief cargo on a ship from Seattle and that they wished to work in coordination with the current President of the Philippines, Mrs. Aquino, to host the vessel.

The reporter told us that President Aquino had responded in a radio broadcast in the Philippines, saying that there was no possible way this "Marcos ship" from Seattle would be permitted into their waters. The reporter called Marcos' aide in Trinidad, who gave him details on the mission and told him that the name of the ship was the "Spirit!" And, he said, now that Aquino had rejected the shipment, the Spirit ship would need to be rerouted to another country.

Sondra listened to what the reporter said, horrified. She asked him to hold on as she ran to find me and bring me to the phone. The reporter repeated his allegations to me.

Of course, I denied the reporter's story in no uncertain terms but, by this time, he was determined to find out if we were a front for a pro-Marcos faction. A few days later I spoke to Paul Dean, the *Los Angeles Times* reporter who was familiar with our operations. Paul was kind enough to phone the reporter in Hawaii to tell him that he was on the wrong track. That almost convinced him to drop the story. However, during the course of their conversation, Paul happened to mention that we had been held up partly because of registration problems.

The reporter from Hawaii called the Coast Guard and found out that we were intending to register Tongan. Now, it just so happened that Marcos had recently been boasting of his friendship with the King of Tonga. It had been reported that he intended to launch a coup against President Aquino from Tonga because of its location in the Pacific, and that he had recently applied for and received a Tongan passport. The reporter called us back to confront us with this new information. This was turning into a real nightmare.

Finally we called the CIA to let them know what was happening and to proclaim our innocence. They assured us that they knew all about us and realized we were not a front for Marcos. Eventually the reporter dropped the story, but by this time our relationship with the Philippine government had become severely compromised.

Then came the exciting morning we were to sail from Pier 66 in Seattle's Puget Sound. We were to launch our first ship in the Lord's navy and that very day He brought in the great white lady "Anastasis", the "Mercy Ships/Youth With a Mission" vessel, to the dock right next to us for a proper send-off. Another ship in God's navy, Anastasis, is a large passenger ship that carries Christian missionaries and medical personnel, providing services, evangelism teams and supplies to many developing nations. We had a great opportunity for fellowship with the crew of the large vessel before we prepared to set sail.

As Gratitude backed out, our volunteer on the dock got anxious and cast off the stern line before he was told to. This caused the stern to swing out toward the Edgewater Hotel. Sondra and I stood on the deck with our hearts pounding and prayed with all our might. Did every move of the Gratitude have to be so hair raising?

Guests at the hotel, accustomed to watching commuter ferries coming in and out on a regular basis, never suspected we weren't in total control. As Gratitude drifted within twenty to thirty feet of their windows before pulling out, they came out on their balconies to wave to us. Finally, as we headed out to sea, with the sound of our friends on the dock singing "Hallelujah to the Lord," both Sondra and I wept and praised God for bringing to fruition a small part of the vision He had given us. The Anastasis blew her loud horn in farewell and approval!

At last, we were operating an international shipping line but, still, on a very slim budget. We had just launched a ship to the Philippines with twenty crew members and only enough fuel to reach San Francisco. We had funds of less than $200 in our entire operation. Still, we owned all that we had, every ship, every piece of equipment, free and clear. We had no debts and owed no one anything. Maybe we were better off than the big ship companies after all.

Each port had generously agreed to give us free short- term moorage and we were working on getting all other services free of charge for the ship in each city. By this time we had managed to get oil pollution insurance, and John Hauff had given us enough fuel to make it to San Francisco. If any port decided not to waive fees or if any other unexpected charge popped up, we were in trouble. Then, of course, there was the need for fuel to enable us to sail from San Francisco to Sacramento, from Sacramento to Los Angeles, from Los Angeles to San Diego, from San Diego to Manila, and from Manila, home. But we felt that the Lord was sending us, so off we went.

Meanwhile, a spirit of fear had descended on the Spirit crew, assisted by one troublesome lady volunteer who had been having meetings at her home to discuss with dissenting crew members the "evils" of our leadership. That spirit of fear succeeded in pulling away about twenty-two of our best crew.

We were upset but didn't have a lot of time to deal with it. We swung back by the Spirit before leaving town, put out what fires we could, then headed out.

In San Francisco, we wanted to get a berth in Fisherman's Wharf where (hopefully) many people would want to tour Gratitude. We figured we'd take a fifty-five gallon drum, paint it red with white letters that said "Donations" and hope people visiting the ship would throw in a dollar or two. In this way, we thought perhaps we could accumulate enough fuel money to sail to Sacramento and so on in each port.

We were upset to be assigned to a berth outside of town, where no one knew we existed. But in the days to come, we were relieved to be tied up at this isolated dock because much of our load arrived in San Francisco. That meant tractor-trailers were pulling in from morning till night and the dock we had been provided had ample space to work, and freedom to maneuver. Had we been at Fisherman's Wharf, it would have been impossible to take on the cargo.

Then, just as we completed loading, the wharfinger called to say that the port needed our pier because the Pope was coming to town and the pier was to be used as a parking lot. Would we mind moving to Fisherman's Wharf? We were delighted. Certainly, Jesus was in control.

San Francisco met us with great warmth. One company came to repair our crew's freezer for no charge, another repaired the Caterpillar engine head for free, a welding company gave us 200 pounds of rod, a sanitation company provided free Porta-Potties and a hospital gave us brand new beds as cargo. We spoke on radio shows and were invited to speak at some local churches. Many people toured and left a dollar here and there. Pretty soon we had accumulated $2,500, enough to buy fuel for Los Angeles.

While in Sacramento, we received a call from a ship broker from Seattle. He had been contacted by a group of men who wanted to purchase Gratitude. He told them we were not likely to sell so they had located a cargo ship in the Bahamas that would be more efficient for our mission and they offered us a trade. We agreed to see the new ship and think it over. Gratitude sailed to the Port of Los Angeles and then on to San Diego. During this time, we awaited news from the group that wanted to trade vessels.

We had thought we'd get press coverage coming into our hometown of Los Angeles. A few TV stations did schedule to greet us at the dock when the ship pulled in at Long Beach. But our plans were not God's plans. That morning a big earthquake hit Los Angeles so no press showed up for us.

A few days later, CNN scheduled to interview us. They had been calling and asking for a story for days and we said okay, but the morning they were to come, the stock market crashed and they were busy elsewhere! So much for publicity.

When we arrived in Los Angeles, the Lord began to put it on my heart that we were to stay and He would develop a warehouse base and office in the Los Angeles area. But, as usual, we had no money, and when the Gratitude sailed on to San Diego, there would only be Sondra, myself and a topless CJ7 jeep.

I phoned a Pastor named Wayne Coombs whom I had met a year back in Seattle at a Full Gospel Businessmen's meeting. He was a pastor at a new church in the wealthy community of Palos Verdes who had said that if I was ever in Los Angeles to give him a call and come to the church and speak. I figured that by this time he would have forgotten me and his invitation, but I called anyway.

He hadn't forgotten; he invited me to speak at the next Sunday morning service. I had never been invited to speak at a Sunday morning church service and was really surprised, but happy, to accept.

During that week, before I spoke, Wayne paid me a visit at the docks. He arrived while I was negotiating a possible trade with local fishermen—our fishing nets for their diesel fuel.

Sunday morning, I drove to his church located atop a hill in affluent Palos Verdes. It was an out-of-use school converted into an elegant sanctuary having a congregation of about 250 people. The worship music sounded beautiful. Wayne talked to his people about the need for an extra generous collection because the rent was due the next day and the church was low on funds. He took the offering, then introduced me.

I spoke, and it seemed that the people were extraordinarily interested in our story. When I was done, Wayne told the congregation about the day that he had visited the ship. He told how he had seen me trying to barter our fish nets for fuel and that just didn't seem right to him. Wayne said he felt like he should take a second offering, which they did.

Then an elder in the church walked forward and whispered something to him. Wayne turned to the congregation, telling them that the man felt the Lord wanted the church to give us both offerings and Wayne agreed! What a shock! I thought I should stand up and object by saying, "The church needs that money for the rent!" But I bit my tongue until the service ended, thinking rather than embarrass anyone, I could just give the money back to the church later.

After the service, people flocked around us to talk. Later, the church staff turned over the offerings. The gift came to more than $15,000! We were astounded! I was still deeply troubled about the church not having enough rent money, feeling like a bandit—coming in to speak and running off with all the loot. But

Wayne assured me that there had been a third offering which turned out to be the biggest one of all. One lady came forward saying that she would be happy to replace the entire offering and then a man behind her said he wouldn't miss out on this blessing. He, too, was going to replace the entire church offering.

I thought to myself, *Lord, I'm not sure of what You're trying to teach me in all this or if there is a lesson, but one thing is for certain, I have a lot to learn about Your ways.*

We had been using our CJ7 jeep (with no top and no doors) for our office. Sondra would drive up and position the jeep in front of a pay phone mounted on a wall at the docks. The booth fit perfectly, right in the empty door space of the jeep. But when the wind blew, her papers would go flying. Also, when a ship began to work its noisy gear, she couldn't hear the party on the other end of the phone. We sure needed a new office because winter was setting in and the clouds were beginning to promise rain.

It was then that Pastor Wayne Coombs called to say that one of the young businessmen in the church wanted to have lunch with me. The following day, Wayne, Loren—the young man from the church—and a man named Will (a friend Wayne was trying to win over to the Lord) arrived to take us to lunch. I took Jamie and Sondra along.

Sondra and I never ate out because we couldn't afford to, so we didn't know where any restaurants were. After driving around a while in the commercial area where our ship was docked, there didn't appear to be any! We were running out of time for our meeting when we passed by a place called "Texas Loosey's." Wayne said, "I hear they have good chili in there," so we all agreed that would be okay. As we entered the restaurant, Pastor Wayne led the way, getting us a booth in the middle of the room.

As we were walking toward it, a pretty young lady passed by. To our great surprise, she appeared to be wearing only two pearl-handled six-guns, a pair of leather riding chaps and American flag tassels hanging from her chest. We slid into our seats as a woman walked up to our table wearing a western outfit that would make even a cowboy blush. She gave us our menus listing "Texas Loosey's" variety of chilis.

I shot a glance over at Pastor Wayne who was seated on the outside edge of the booth. There he was, the lead culprit, the pastor who had led us into this den. His face looked like a bowl of red cherries.

It was an interesting task for us to try to ignore the women who strolled around the tables (seeing they were dressed in lingerie right out of an old French novel). Seems there was a lingerie show there that day and they were selling off their garments, right then and there. Wayne picked up a large menu and held it tightly to his face. He was trying to hold back a great howl of laughter from behind his menu. He couldn't even speak.

I thought, *Dear God, here we are, three novice missionaries, a young man we are trying to lead to the Lord, a young entrepreneur financier of the church and the big kahuna, Pastor Wayne Coombs himself, in a chili strip-joint being invited to a pajama party.*

We set aside the events at hand and ordered lunch. Settling in, we began to talk about the great and mighty God we served and the miracles that He'd performed. We had mentioned in the church meeting a couple of days earlier that the Gratitude was sailing onto San Diego for additional loading. We were later to recognize that this unusual meeting in a port town, which we originally considered a stopover, was God's timing. There we were in a strange environment, hostile to the kingdom of God, but it was there, even in a place like "Texas Loosey's", that another great miracle, perhaps one of the greatest yet, began to unfold.

Loren told us an interesting story of how his business had been blessed and how he had to move to a larger warehouse. He had six months left on the lease of his old building and had been dealing with a neighboring businessman who wanted to take over the lease. Loren described his neighbor Tim as a tough businessman. They had a serious disagreement over price and terms of the lease.

The warehouse was in a nice part of town. Loren mentioned that he had heard me say while I was speaking at church that we needed a warehouse in which to store supplies for the Spirit when she came down the coast. He said he had decided to continue to pay on the lease ($5,000 a month) and give it to us free of charge, if we wanted it. It was only for six months, Loren said, but he knew that God would do something else for us after that.

After lunch, we slipped out of the booth and wove our way through the six-guns and cowboys hats. As we closed the front door behind us, I looked back over my shoulder at the big star of Texas with the words below: "Texas Loosey's—Best Chili in Town." How would I ever explain to anyone that God surely must have been with us in a place like this? I could hardly believe it myself. The miracle of a warehouse—the warehouse that God told us He would provide—beginning in a place like "Texas Loosey's." Still, I myself had no idea of the scope of what lay ahead, of the outreach that was to grow and result in thousands and thousands of souls being saved.

11

GOD'S STOREHOUSE/
FREE FOOD—WE DELIVER

Later that day, we drove to the new warehouse. Just as Loren had described, it was located in a beautiful area just a few blocks from the ocean on 190th Street in Redondo Beach. This building was nothing like we expected when we thought "warehouse." The beautiful stucco building, standing proudly behind wrought iron gates had a large fenced parking lot and huge roll-up doors. Inside, seven lovely offices with heaters, telephones and a telex awaited our use. We could buzz each other on the intercom from room to room. After years of living with inoperable ship toilets and dock-side Porta-Potty heads, we were thrilled to have two small restrooms with toilets that actually flushed.

We moved in right away, sleeping on the lush carpet floors and turning on the heaters for warmth at night. We cooked in a large closet and used a small sink in the ladies' restroom to clean our pots and pans. In order for us to "shower", we used the sink in the men's room to take a sponge bath. Life was great.

As Jamie and Debi Saunders headed the crew sailing Gratitude on to San Diego, Sondra, Ray and I made this mansion of a warehouse our new home. Loren was generous in every way. The Lord definitely showed us His love, not only by His words but by His actions.

We were convinced (now that God had given us a warehouse) that cargo for the ship would begin to pour in. What a disappointment as week after week, in spite of all of our diligent efforts, the warehouse remained virtually empty. We could sweep the floor from one end to the other. I didn't know what to think, knowing we were in the right place at the right time, going in the right direction, but still, there seemed to be no blessing on the warehouse.

Soon we would be out of the warehouse and back into our CJ7 jeep. Loren would have put out $30,000 plus and it would only have provided a dry shelter for three people. This just couldn't be God. I knew there must be something I wasn't hearing. Searching my soul, I thought, *Lord, how did we miss it? What did we do wrong?*

One afternoon, I announced to Sondra, "Grab a notebook and a pencil. Come across the street to the Cimmarron Restaurant. We're gonna have some coffee and God is going to tell us what He wants us to do." Time was running out and I was convinced God would speak now.

We walked into the restaurant and took the big booth by the window. We ordered coffee. Then Sondra looked at me and said, "Okay, I'm ready." Suddenly, I knew exactly what He wanted us to do. As I thought it over, the idea seemed completely insane. I didn't think that anyone in his right mind would even consider doing such a wild, irresponsible thing.

Hesitantly, looking at Sondra, I began, "I'm almost afraid to tell you what we are going to do next. Our church friends will probably say, "Those ship people with their presumptuous 'faith' have finally gone too far." Critics who predicted that we could never keep up this system of believing God for everything, will think now that they were absolutely right all along."

By appearances they were correct. There had been no donation of fuel for Gratitude's mission to the Philippines, and the crew aboard Spirit had dwindled to a faithful few. The tugboat was being guarded by only one man and no cargo was coming in anywhere. The ship mission seemed to have come to a complete standstill, with no way out and little provision.

But, nevertheless, this is what I felt God was telling us to do. I told Sondra, "Write this down. We're going to expand and start a whole new outreach having nothing to do with what God has already given us."

It flashed through my mind, *God, could this really be you?* But I knew it had to be God. I would never do anything **this** **absurd** on my own!

I continued, "We're going to put an ad in a Los Angeles newspaper, in this big city with poverty all around. It's going to read something like this, 'Are your children hungry? Are you out of work or elderly? Free food! We deliver.'

"Then we're going to get out a big map of the area and when people call in, we're going to take their names, their addresses and find out how many people are in their family. We're going to stick a pin in the map to mark where they live. We'll keep taking phone calls until we have pins all over the map.

"Then we'll take out the yellow pages and look for churches in the area where the pins are located. We'll call the churches and tell them that there are men and women with children that are hungry and hurting, who have called us. We'll tell the church people that, 'We'll gather up the food, put it into sacks and give it to you if you would simply take the food to these needy families in your own neighborhood.' When you deliver it, tell them, 'These provisions are from the Lord.' Tell them that you love and care for them. Perhaps you can hand them Sunday school stories for their children and explain how the Lord loves them, how He cares. Invite them to attend your church, and maybe offer to pray a blessing on the household, that the Lord would change the circumstances that put them in this bad situation." These are hurting families, the kind the Word tells us about, the kind of people the Bible says He wants us to care for.

I see it, Lord. It was beginning to become clear to me. I understood that people could actually get up out of their pews and take food to their neighborhood, not to knock cold on a door, uninvited, but to knock on a family's door which has asked for help. The occupants would be waiting for them to arrive because the church members would be delivering groceries for the children.

I could see what a great opportunity this would be for the people in the church to begin to show love by their actions. A needy man sees the newspaper has a number to call that's offering free food. Lo and behold, the number turns out to be that of his neighborhood church! I realized that the church would get the credit, and God would get the glory!

A man we knew, an artist, offered to design the ad. Another said he'd place it. A few days later, the phone began to ring like a musical instrument. Our mouths were tired from talking, our fingers sore from taking the food orders. Now all we needed were bags to hold the groceries, trucks to gather up all the food, and food for all the bags.

Ray was busy driving downtown on a continuous search for food with his red Volkswagen bus, the blessing of the Lord all over him. He would find and pick up so much food that the bus could not contain it. He drove back and forth from L.A. as fast as he could, filling that bus full of food. The food he shoved inside was so heavy that the tires splayed out in all directions. Sometimes all we could see was Ray's shining face sandwiched in among great piles of food as he beamed with excitement about all the items he had retrieved from an uncertain fate.

About this time, a man named Bob Steward befriended us. He was a tall handsome guy with a beautiful wife named Betty, who had been a state champion in the Miss America contest. Bob helped the food program get started by volunteering his time to call local churches and offer to enlist them. In the years that followed, Bob has remained a strong and faithful part of this program.

We had no grocery bags in which to put the food items and no money to purchase them. So we went to individual markets and asked them for any seconds or overages of grocery bags they might have. We explained what we were doing and they responded by giving us stacks and stacks of bags.

Food continued to come in as fast as Ray could pick it up, each load increasing in quality. Also, more and more Christians came to help sort, prepare and sack each week's food.

One afternoon, Wayne Coombs, with his great heart of mercy, came to the warehouse to see his church members helping the poor. As he strolled through the warehouse, he stopped and turned to me. With his right hand, he dropped his gold-rimmed Porsche prescription turbo sunglasses to the end of his nose. Peering over them, he said, "Now listen Don, this is a great thing you're doing, but level with me. What is the thing that you're most in need of right now?"

I thought to myself, *Lord, thank you.* This was a proper question at a proper time. "Wayne, as you know, we gather produce all week and deliver to homes on Saturday through all these churches, but we're in serious need of a refrigeration unit to store the vegetables to give them a longer shelf life."

Wayne smiled, put his glasses back into place, and said, "Done! Order the thing." The refrigeration unit arrived, and the food outreach surged forward as Ray raced faster and faster in his little red Volkswagen.

Then Tom Miller stopped by to see us. Tom was a precious friend I had known for years—a good Christian man who sincerely loved the Lord. He had a large horse ranch in Covina, California—a competition show stable.

For years he and I competed, at his ranch in Covina, at mine in Malibu and then at the polo club on Sunset Boulevard. He saw the real change in my life and was taken with my effort to serve God. After his visit, Tom stopped at a truck dealership where he saw a handsome flatbed with a lift gate. He knew this was the truck we needed. He told the dealer about what we were doing and asked about the price. The man said, "That truck is not for sale."

"Not for sale?" Tom asked. "Why not?"

"Because I'm going to give it to them myself!" the man said.

Tom called me right away and told me what happened. He said, "The man wants to give you a truck. You better come to pick it up right away!"

I rushed over to the dealership. By the time I arrived, the dealer, Andy Anderson, had decided to give us two trucks! Now when Ray went to collect up the food, they could bring it out to him with forklifts by the pallet load.

The poor and needy kept calling. We heard sounds of hungry children in the background; sometimes even the children themselves called. But, to our dismay, as we phoned churches to tell them there were children without food living in their area, an average of eight out of every ten churches would tell us they weren't interested, giving us responses like, "We don't have that sort in this church...We're too busy with our own activities...We don't have poor in this neighborhood...Our members would be uncomfortable with that kind of person here."

After a time, an unexpected thing began to take place. In each church, there are the precious handful, you know them— the "doers"—the old man who sets up the projector, the person no one notices, the quiet guy that drives the church van, the woman who stays late to help put everything away, the parking lot attendant who stands outside in any kind of weather to make sure everybody else makes it into the church. You know the kind, the great ones that nobody talks about, the great ones that are taken for granted. We discovered that this group seemed to have their own secret group of friends.

It worked like this: One of those guys with their trooper wives would show up at the warehouse, having heard about the program from other volunteers, and would help bag up food. When it was time to deliver, we'd call out the addresses of people who churches hadn't yet "adopted", and these new arrivals would say, "That's my area, let me deliver that bag." Joyfully loading their cars up with food, they would drive off and minister to people as they delivered the groceries. They found that even if people didn't receive the Lord on the first week's visit, the needy would be ministered to by the food all week long as they ate the Holy Spirit-anointed gifts.

Then, the following Saturday, there on the doorstep of the needy family would appear the beautiful feet of the precious man with the groceries. Again food was given to feed their children. The visitor was always prepared to pray a blessing on their household, that the Lord would find them work, would help break addictions, would bring them new hope through the love of Jesus.

Often, throughout the week, the Holy Spirit would deal with this family. The parents would become convicted because their children were not attending Sunday School. Where do you suppose they thought to go as they remembered the beautiful face of the man from the local church who had been there on their doorstep, faithful in his deeds?

Suddenly that church would begin to fill up with all sorts of wonderful new families. Some Pastors would wonder, "How did you find our chapel?" Many replied, "It was because of the kind man who brought food and led us to the Lord!"

So the program grew. Now with large trucks, Ray made runs to the downtown L.A. produce wholesalers and to the charity dock. Distributors brought out pallet after pallet to load into our trucks, sometimes whole loads at one stop.

Ray collected tons of nutritious fresh fruits and vegetables—beautiful food, at no charge. Bakeries began to bake extra bread just for us. Some even began to deliver. We were given pies, cakes and pastries, often by the truckload.

After a short ninety days, the program grew to the point that we were distributing enough supplemental food to provide 60,000 meals a week and more—every week.

We saw so clearly that God's heart is soft to the poor as each and every week and each and every day, His supply was bountiful. We gathered up the cardboard boxes in which the food was given to us. We stored them up all week and sold them to recycling paper plants to fuel our trucks.

Warehouse and food distribution on 190th street in Redondo Beach

Ray George

Debi and Jamie Saunders

Mechanics came to fix our trucks without charge. Tire shops fixed our tires for free. All our needs were met! Amazingly, the entire food operation ran at just about no cost.

Good things too numerous to mention continued to pour in— and have continued even now, years later. Fifty-two weeks a year, God remains faithful—not just one or two holidays a year but **every single day!** He is a God we can count on.

Then we began meeting people from corporations that had overages of perfectly good cereal, soup and other items, and didn't want to pay warehouse taxes on them. They'd explain that they didn't want us to give it out in the local area because they couldn't afford to destabilize their company by flooding the market with their reserves. But, if we would agree to take it **out** of the country and distribute it in foreign lands, then they would give it all to us free of charge.

These companies told us that often, to dispose of their goods—even those in perfect condition—they would hire trucks to haul it to the local landfill, paying healthy sums to bury it. They said it would be good for morale in the company if their employees saw that their surplus products were not going to waste, but were instead going to help people. It would make their employees feel secure, they said, to know that they worked for a company with a good heart, strong and benevolent, and that their work was going to a good cause.

So, you see, the blessing of God began to fall on the ship operation through feeding the local poor. The Lord began filling the warehouse for our overseas projects, too. He began to show me how we were to give out food all over the world in the same way that we gave it away locally.

I began to understand that when our ships started arriving in Central America, or elsewhere, it would be of no real purpose for the people to think that all the food and supplies came from a warehouse in Los Angeles.

We were to remain in the background, letting the churches receive the credit, and God would establish His glory. In this way, we would not be building our own kingdom. We didn't need to. God would still supply our own needs. Our efforts would be in building the only kingdom of value—the kingdom of the living God.

To this day, our warehouses don't bear our name or even a sign. Our trucks are painted plain. With no way for people to know where they're from, they come and go in silence, offering all the credit to the local pastors and their church.

Week after week, year after year, volunteers by the hundreds continue to show up on Saturday to bag and distribute food. We're never quite sure where they come from or why they decide to join us that particular Saturday morning. One week it will be the boy scouts, the next week a fraternity, then the girl scouts or maybe even a sorority or two. Then, out of nowhere, a big church group will turn up. When we ask, "How did you know we needed your help today?" They might say, "People told us that we could come here and help whenever we want, that we don't need to call." And so they come, always on a day when God knows we need them. He always supplies just the right number of volunteers.

I remember one young man who drove up in his Volkswagen bug, surfboard atop. He said, "Hey man, the surf is up and I was on my way to the beach with nothing but the waves on my mind. Then suddenly I felt **compelled** to turn the car back and come here to bag groceries."

He looked to me for an answer. I pointed to the end of the line and said, "Take yourself over there with all those other compelled people and sack groceries!" Yes, it amazes me even today, after all these years, that workers never fail to show up just when we need them.

This exciting program is not successful because of money, endorsements or invitations. It isn't based on wise business practices, powerful men or the great eloquence of our own speaking. I boast that it's based only on the undeniable, absolute, true Word of our God.

12

SOMEBODY UP THERE LIKES ME

After loading Gratitude with all that we could store—hospital beds, medical supplies and dehydrated food—we found that we couldn't load the ship as heavy as was needed to get her to sit deep enough in the water to be safe to cross the Pacific to the Philippines.

Everything we attempted in order to add more weight to it just wasn't adequate. We realized that the Gratitude could not be loaded heavily enough with the light, mercy-type cargo that we were carrying (designed as she was to carry fish and water in her tanks). Hospital beds simply did not displace the same weight as water. Our mission (we had to admit) was to save lives, not take them.

We realized that although we may be able to make a mission or two with this ship, it would be best if we traded or sold her. For this reason, we were strongly considering the offer to trade for a smaller cargo ship in Miami that came through a Seattle ship broker. What we didn't know (and what the broker didn't divulge) was that Gratitude's market value was soaring tremendously every month.

Someone blessed us with round trip tickets to visit the Spirit in Seattle. We hadn't been there in several months and wanted to encourage our crew who had continued to work faithfully on the ship.

We found the crew getting along fine. They were picking up leftover barbecued chicken and rib dinners from a local restaurant each night. They continued to feed hundreds of people who lived on the streets, also giving food to numerous ministries.

Faithful crew members Big George, Scott, Pete and his wife, Jan, were holding down the fort. We met great new crew members for the first time—the Labbe family who had come from Connecticut and Colleen McBride from upstate New York. Colleen proved to be a faithful, intelligent and capable woman who couldn't boil water. (Somehow she was immediately assigned to the galley.)

The new additions to the crew blessed us. However, there was a bit of depression on board over the lack of several six-inch water valves needed for piping in the main engine fire pumps.

For a long time, the crew had been praying for these valves. Used, they sold for more than $1500 apiece. They had to be special gate valves to hold up against the salt water, with brass interior and stainless steel stems. It was a tall order; I just didn't see a way we could obtain them.

For some reason, we hadn't thought to take them from the Rose Knot before she was sold. Sondra and I had exhausted every lead. The weekend approached with no valves in sight, and by now, we, too, were genuinely depressed. I told Sondra, "Let's just board one of the ferries, pay our fare and ride the boat back and forth all day. I want to ride on a boat that is actually going somewhere."

Sondra shook her head, "Don, I don't want anything to do with riding on a boat. But, I'd really like to walk in the forest. That's something we haven't done in years."

"Tell you what," I offered. "We'll compromise. Let's get on one of the ferries. We'll ride across to Bainbridge Island where we can go for a walk in the forest."

"Oh, that sounds good," Sondra agreed.

We took the ferry across the bay to the island, got off at Winslow where the forest runs down to the water's edge. It's a truly beautiful place, with Canadian geese honking, mallards swimming all around and beautiful pathways winding through the woods. We began our walk.

It had been raining, as it often does in Seattle, and the ground was soft and muddy. As we made our way down through a wooded park, Sondra suddenly slipped. Her feet flew out from under her and she landed smack in the middle of a big mud puddle. She happened to be wearing brand new white pants that the Lord had provided for her, only now they were splattered with an ugly shade of brown mud. She slowly got to her feet, mud all over her back side and down her legs.

"I'm a mess! Just look at me!" she cried.

I felt so bad for her. She loved those white pants, and now she'd have to ride on the ferry all the way home in muddy, wet slacks. I wanted to do something to help, so I asked her for her scarf and told her to wait there on the path. "I'll go see if I can find some water to dip the scarf in. Maybe I can wipe some of the mud off. I'll be back as soon as I can."

I carefully made my way down the side of the grass hill into the back of an old shipyard, looking around for something that may have caught the rain. There were lots of old parts and equipment lying around. Finding a round, cup-like thing holding water, I quickly soaked the scarf in it and turned to hurry back, knowing that Sondra was waiting patiently on the path.

As I took a step, a loud, deep voice spoke to me out of nowhere. "What was that?" the voice asked. I stopped in my tracks, looking around to see who had spoken to me. I didn't see anyone, but somebody was there. I heard 'em. I took another step up the hill. The voice rang out again, this time louder and clearer: "What was that you dipped your rag in?"

I turned around and said out loud, "I don't know. Who is it? Who's here?"

There was no answer. Whether the voice actually spoke out loud or came from inside my head, I really don't know for sure. Either way, it was clear that there was no one around.

Walking back over to where I'd dipped the rag, I looked down at the pallet of parts. Amazed, I realized that right in front of me on this pallet were **six-inch valves with stainless steel stems and brass interior**. I blurted out, "That's just what we're looking for!"

Not just one, but pallet after pallet held those six-inch valves. I couldn't believe it. Dropping Sondra's water soaked scarf, I raced straight to the shipyard office.

It was Russ Trask's shipyard, where we were once moored. I knew Russ well—a tough businessman—but I decided to approach him straight out. I said, "Russ you have some pallets of six-inch valves, and I'm in bad need of them."

He laughed. "You need 'em bad, do you? Something you gotta have? Sounds like I got you just where I want you."

I held my hands up as if I were being robbed. "It's true, Russ. I'm in a fix. "

"Well now, those valves are high dollar items and in good demand. What you got to trade me for 'em?" he asked.

I was out of answers. "I don't have anything that you'd be interested in that I don't desperately need."

"That's not what I hear. I hear you got a donation load of canned salmon, and I got a taste for canned salmon."

It was true that we had gotten in several tons of canned salmon, so I confessed, "Yes, we do have canned salmon."

Russ stared at me with a hard business look. "Here's my deal. Take it or leave it. Drop me off a couple of cases of that canned salmon and take as many valves as you need."

I walked out of the office in a daze, stopping again by the valves to pick up Sondra's scarf from the ground.

I thought, *Let me take a moment to figure out what has just happened here. Don't let this one just pass me by Lord.*

First: We've been praying for weeks for six-inch valves. Today, we're all depressed with no solution in sight. I get so down that I think I need a ride on a ferry boat. Sondra thinks she needs a walk in the forest (in white slacks).

Next: We get on the ferryboat and go to the island. We depart the ferryboat and begin a walk in the forest. We're walking on the path overlooking the valves.

"We finally got them here," the angels of provision must have said to one another. "We got them off the Spirit ship, onto the ferry boat, into the forest and down the path. Oh no, they're walking past the valves without a second look." We stroll right by. Something has to be done.

Then, all of a sudden, "Oops!" Sondra slides or trips and falls down the hill right into the middle of a mud puddle. A bright idea out of nowhere pops into my head. "Take her scarf and find something that has collected the rain and wipe her off, Sir Galahad." Down the hill I go, her little scarf in hand. Looking down, I spy some metal trough holding water.

"Ah," the angels must have thought, "We finally have them where we want them," as they present me with dozens of six-inch valves. I'm actually dipping the scarf inside a valve but, instead of noticing, I turn to walk away!

I can hear the angels saying now, "Oh no, we've brought him all the way here. He's dunked her scarf in the very valve! But now this guy is going back up the hill, not even realizing what he's just had his hand in." There is nothing else they can do but resort to audio.

So they call out, "What was that?" I keep walking. They continue: "What was that you dipped your rag in?" Finally, I go back over and discover the valves.

How did Russ Trask find out we had a load of canned salmon?

Isn't it amazing—we pray for things and then have to be run over with the answer like a truck before we recognize God's response. I began to understand the effort God must expend to make our provisions.

I could see Sondra on the side of the hill, still waiting patiently. She felt 100% better when I told her the wonderful thing that had just happened. Still all muddy, but excited, she couldn't wait to come back with us in the truck and watch with her own amazed eyes as we gathered up the valves.

13

MIRACLES ON 190TH STREET

The food ministry became a great joy to us but, still, we were undergoing one of the most stressful times of our lives.

The ship ministry had come to a dead stop, and our hearts were heavy. People who were counting on us to bring supplies to the Philippines called to see why we hadn't delivered; most were understanding. They knew we had offered to go free of charge and that we were trusting God for all the provisions. But some were angry and called up with serious accusations against our character.

Half of our friends were saying that the food program was obviously what God wanted us to do because He was blessing it. They said that we should forget the ships. Our other friends said we had been distracted by the food program and were forgetting about our true calling, the ships.

But we were not distracted and we did not forget. Every waking moment, we ate, drank, breathed the ships and wondered at our failure. In our hearts we knew that giving up the ships was impossible. We didn't understand what mistake we'd made or why we were going through this humiliation, but we knew the Lord had not forgotten us and, that one day, the ships would sail.

The ship broker from Seattle continued to call, telling us of one deal after another, none of which materialized. Jamie flew with one of our captains to take a look at the small freighter in Miami. The ship was beautiful and well maintained, but very small. We were aware they had overpriced the vessel but it didn't seem to matter because they wanted to make a straight trade with our ship. As months passed, however, the buyers were unable to follow through on the deal.

We had trusted the broker, who had been presented to us as a good Christian man. We took his word that he had qualified the buyers and that they had the ability to make and close the deal for Gratitude. But repetitive broken promises of an impending sale or exchangé helped break the spirit of the crew. One after another lost faith and left, including the captain, who began looking into getting his own ship. The only crew who remained were the Saunders; they were faithful and true.

This time in the ministry was so hard that Sondra and I wondered if God was happy with us at all.

One afternoon we were daydreaming about how things could be when the ships began to sail. I said, "Wouldn't it be nice if we had lots of new shirts for the crew? Maybe they should be white polo shirts so when they go into town or we had visitors aboard, the crew would look sharp. And we need some new thick jersey T-shirts and maybe some Russell sweats, the brand that's extra heavy cotton—warm, toasty and never seem to wear out." (Russell sweat clothes were a favorite of mine, a special quality I regularly bought at a time long past when cost was not a concern.)

Of course, no one overheard our conversation, nor did we mention it to anyone else. Yet, a couple of days later, a United Parcel Service van arrived with eighteen large crates. We helped the driver unload, signed for the boxes and asked what was inside. "I don't know. The paperwork should be in one of the crates," he said and drove away.

We cracked open the top of the first crate. Incredibly, it was stacked full of beautiful white polo shirts of various sizes. We pulled some out of the box and looked them over. They were very good quality, 100% cotton. We opened another case. It too had beautiful top quality white polo shirts.

Incredulous, we continued to crack open the crates. The next one contained cotton jersey T-shirts, just as I had described, the thick ones that really last. We couldn't believe our eyes. More and more T-shirts, more and more polo shirts. We opened another crate which was stacked to the top with Russell sweat shirts. We were in total disbelief! Was there a hidden microphone? Was someone listening to our soft whispering and smallest desires?

Someone was listening. Someone was taking notes. Someone was collecting and gathering, folding and stacking, boxing and crating. Someone was sending and delivering.

Because there in front of us was our soft whisper that had become a reality, even to the styles, sizes and brands. This was no coincidence. This was our Father's love.

At this time in Los Angeles, food was limited to mostly fruits, vegetables and breads. The Spirit ship in Seattle was taking in chicken and ribs. The crew was feeding thousands of people while doing repairs. The tugboat Reverence was stocked and loaded with dry stores. The Gratitude had plenty of food to take to the Philippine Islands, but in Los Angeles we were dreaming of meat.

We were living in the warehouse, sleeping on the floor. Sondra was cooking on a hot plate in a closet. Sometimes we would walk down the street to a supermarket, stroll down the aisles looking at the canned string beans and creamed corn, and through the deli section to gaze at the cottage cheese and bologna. Then we'd walk down toward the aroma of the bakery and into the section where people were buying steaks, chickens, all sorts of fresh meats. We would hear other people busily shopping and making remarks to each other like, "I think we'll have steak" or "I'm tired of steak, let's have chicken." We'd overhear others saying, "It's Friday, let's have fish and a roast on Saturday." We had ships in ports up and down the Pacific Coast worth millions of dollars. We fed hundreds of people a week and gave them clothes. But here we were sleeping on a warehouse floor, strolling through a supermarket, window shopping.

Sondra looked at the chicken, whispering, "That sure looks good."

"Wish we had some sirloin steaks," I said. But wish as we

would, we headed home empty-handed.

Three days later, a woman pulled in with cases of plump whole chickens. She asked, "Would you have any need for these?"

"Oh I think we could figure out something to do with them," we confessed. "We know some hungry people."

I watched Sondra, not much of a cook, as she stood in the closet wielding a large knife, hacking away at these poor little chickens. *"I don't mean to complain, Lord,"* she said, but maybe next time you could send them already cut up in parts.

The following day, the same woman who had given us the chickens came by with another load, only these were parts— thighs, legs and breasts. She gave us seventy pounds. I was a little jealous. I distinctly remembered saying that I'd like some sirloin and, as yet, I hadn't seen one piece of cow come out of that lady's truck. Then the woman stunned us both. She pulled out some cases of sirloin steaks. "Can I drop a couple of these to you?" she asked.

God, who could believe this? Only we know how much You love us, Lord.

Who was standing there with us? Who was listening to even our smallest wishes? Who was taking notes?

❖❖❖

One day in Seattle, just before Easter, crew member Steve Kingery was working the food route. We had a large Ford van that we used to make a daily run all over Seattle picking up food of many types. Some stops would give us pies, cakes and pastries. Another stop would give fruits and vegetables. Another would give us meats and fish, some prepared and some fresh. We'd generally take a good part of the day to collect all the food items that came in on a daily basis. There would always be large portions from one place or another.

Easter week was hardly an exception and usually abundant. Steve had the van parked near the gangway, ready to set off on the run. He waved good-bye and was about to head off down the ramp when one of the galley crew called to him. "Steve, we have berries and cake for Easter dinner and we want to make strawberry short cake, but we have no whipped cream. Make sure you bring home whipped cream."

Steve shook his head, knowing that we had never gotten any whipped cream. Another cook laughingly called out, "Oh, Steve, pick up some Easter lilies at the store, too. We want them for the table."

Steve scoffed as he walked down the gangway. "They want Easter lilies and whipped cream!"

Strangely enough, for the very first time, each store Steve visited that day had nothing for us. At the last market, usually the biggest stop, the manager said, "Steve, I'm so sorry, we usually have so much but today we have nothing—oh, except that case of whipped cream and those Easter Lilies!"

Steve couldn't believe his ears. "Whipped cream and Easter lilies?" He gathered up the crates in disbelief and excitedly returned to the ship. Needless to say, the galley crew was ecstatic.

Someone was listening. Someone cared, even enough to eliminate every other item from the route except whipped cream and Easter lilies, just so there could be no doubt of this very special "coincidence."

❖❖❖

One Saturday morning in early March, Tim, the businessman who ran a very large and successful shirt company next door to our warehouse, came by with his architect to check out his new area—clipboard and pad in hand. His company was scheduled to take over our space in May. His business was growing and he badly needed the expansion area.

We were busy sacking and loading groceries that morning. Tim and the architect strolled through, making suggestions of various structural changes in the walls and doorways. Tim gestured and said, "I need to blow this out and put a door there, a passageway through this direction, perhaps another window over there."

He saw me and asked if I was the man in charge. Tim was all business and very direct. He said, "Listen, my business is very pressed and we need this space right away, as we have construction here to do. So what would it take, I mean, how much would it cost me? What's the bottom line? How much are we talking here for you to move out early?"

I explained that we had, as of yet, found nothing else and had nowhere to go. Alarmed, he replied, "I've got to have this place. You can't mean you're not going to be out of here when you're supposed to be?"

"No," I said. "I mean we have nowhere to move early, but we will be out of here on time, out of your way. We won't be any trouble to you."

Then he asked, "What is this stuff? Who are you? Some kind of a produce man or something?"

It was my opportunity to explain who we were and what we did, how the food changed peoples' lives, how the poor ate and how the children appreciated it. As I spoke to him, his countenance began to change. There was a kindness and softness that wasn't there before. A tear begin to form. He was so fresh and direct. "You know, what you do here is so vastly more important than my T-shirts and what we do. My wife and I couldn't take this away from you." He paused, then continued, "You go ahead and stay here. I'll pay the bill." For eighteen months we stayed and Tim paid all the bills!

In mid-1989, it became necessary for us to move to a new warehouse facility. Tim had overcrowded his operation to the point that we could no longer bear to see him sacrifice the space we occupied.

We found a warehouse at Berth 57 in the Port of Los Angeles where warehouse vacancies were almost nonexistent. The specific building we wanted was not available but, fortunately, one directly next to it had some space. We had received a small down payment on the Gratitude from another set of potential buyers, so we rented the warehouse quickly before it was lost. The down payment had allowed us to pay off some debts and move into the warehouse, but it took almost all our cash to pay two months as a security deposit and the first month's rent.

Our first day at the warehouse, I was on the docks with a fire hose washing down the receiving area. I was empty inside, hurting, and had been up the night before with a terrible stomach ache. I knew that I'd not stepped out in faith. I'd not asked God's permission, I had just gone and signed the lease, making a solid business deal based on my needs. I had taken it out of His hands. It was total presumption on my part.

Oh, no, I thought, *God's going to get me now. I just know it. I had finally made a really bad mistake. I better prepare for this beating I'm about to receive.* But instead of a beating, up drove Loren, the original donor of the warehouse in Redondo Beach, with a huge smile on his face.

Excitedly, he greeted me. "Hi, Don. I have great news."

I turned off the hose. "What is it, Loren?"

He said, "Last night, God woke me up and spoke to me."

"Wow, He spoke to you right out? What did He say?"

Loren was so excited, I knew it must be something really great. Loren replied, "The Lord said, 'Loren, why is Don up tonight with a stomach ache, worrying about his bills?' 'I don't know, Lord,' I said, 'Why is Don up tonight worrying over his bills?'

"The Lord replied, 'It's Don's job to feed the hungry and clothe the poor. It's your job, Loren, to pay the bills.'"

Loren laughed. "Send the bills to me, little buddy. I'll pay 'em all," he said and drove off down the street.

I walked over and sat on the dock with my head down. "Lord, at this moment, I should be overjoyed and praising You, but instead I'm ashamed. I was prepared for the beating I thought You were going to give me. I didn't know how much You loved us."

As I sat there in tears, my head down, I felt the warmth and the love of God, and His presence surrounded me as He ministered His love.

Everything prospered at the new warehouse facility. The food ministry increased to over 100,000 meals a week and kept growing. The building sat jammed to the rafters, full to capacity and beyond with relief supplies.

The fire department team would arrive for a routine inspection and cringe. The chief would say, "Clean everything up. I'll be back in three days." But because he knew what we were doing and didn't want to cause us trouble, we wouldn't see him for another year.

The electric meter reader would come and complain that he couldn't find the meter. The man who serviced the fire extinguishers would stop by to renew them for us free of charge. God provided everything.

We gave supplies away but also stored up for the first mission of the Spirit. Cargo came in so fast we couldn't keep track of it.

We got an opportunity to send eleven truckloads to the Philippines on a commercial ship. *Glory to God!* I thought. *We'll dig out all that we can; we'll make aisles and be able to see what we have in here.*

Excitedly, we begin to load all eleven containers as fast as we could. But as we loaded, the Lord demonstrated the principal of giving and receiving. As we finished the last container and closed the door, the warehouse was more jammed than when we began. You see, as we loaded out eleven truckloads, thirteen more came in.

When you give in the Lord's name, it comes back, pressed down and running over. Giving invokes the law of return. The biblical concept of giving and receiving is a law, like the law of gravity, and we realized then that what we were going to need, very soon, was a much bigger warehouse.

14

FEAR NOT

Finally, the time came when the Lord revealed the reason Gratitude was not allowed to complete her mission. Looking back, we realized that the ship was not ideal for our purpose, yet an issue much more important than that caused all our delays.

We had sailed the ship, in faith, from one port to the next with only enough fuel to make that port, but none to sail on to the next—no funds in the bank and no security, except in Him.

But a week or two before we left Seattle, nearly everyone had approached me, asking for my word that we wouldn't leave the shores of the U.S. for the Philippines without complete provisions for the **entire** trip.

Most of the conversations went something like this (one-on-one and very private): "Don, I understand that you like to trust God and do things in simple faith, but we're worried that you're going to jump out and do something that might bring disaster upon us. Would you give me your word that you won't sail off across the sea with all these people before we have what we need? It's one thing to trust God for ships, boats, food, people and all those miracles while we're safely here in America. It's quite another to sail off across the ocean with only the provisions to get to the next stop."

They were worried I would take some "foolish" leap of faith. I felt grieved, realizing they must not have considered me much of a leader, probably thinking I was some sort of a nut. Suddenly, it became important to me that the crew think I was a capable leader so, on impulse, I called them all together to make an announcement. "So that you all know that I am dealing with a full deck, we have no intention of leaving the shores or the safety of the U.S. for foreign lands without full provisions for the entire trip."

Sighs filled the room, and I could sense relief throughout the crew. Now they were happy and ready to go. But my spirit felt heavy with the knowledge that I may have made a very grave mistake. That decision went against everything God had taught me in the past two years. My eyes were off the Lord; instead I had listened to the voices of men, drawing a line in the sand. In essence, I had told the Lord: "This far and no farther until You provide."

God's great miracles had followed us all the way down the coast as He had provided everything we'd needed from Seattle to San Diego. But once in San Diego, it was as if someone turned off a giant faucet and the provision stopped. The favor was gone, the crew left and the ship was nearly abandoned. I realize now, with full understanding, that the miraculous provisions for Gratitude would never have stopped. God would have provided the next needs of the ship upon our arrival in Hawaii, the first leg of the transpacific crossing to the Philippines.

I'm ashamed to admit this was a hard lesson, an expensive one that cost us a ship. (The Gratitude never went to sea for us.) When I draw a line, God is a gentleman and won't force my will. Thankfully though, because of His great grace and forgiving nature, He took this calamity and turned it into a major blessing.

The months had slipped by and conditions in the fishing industry transformed. As a result of new regulations enacted by the U.S. Government, American-built tuna super-seiners like Gratitude were suddenly in great demand.

During a recent seven-year lull in the business, most of these ships had been converted to work in other types of fishing. Gratitude was one of the few American-built super-seiners left and her fair market value was soaring.

We began to look for buyers on our own and, in August of 1989, we sold Gratitude to an American-Japanese firm for a price more than twenty times what Paul Watson had paid for her. We received that amount minus some foreign brokerage fees, and with this boost of funds, we were able to kick the ship ministry into high gear.

We unloaded the cargo from Gratitude and shipped it to the Philippines on commercial carriers. As soon as we sold the ship, we transferred Jamie and Debi Saunders to Seattle to prepare the great ship Spirit for a long-awaited dry dock. Then I flew to Seattle in order to arrange a date at the shipyard.

Unimar Dry Dock was hesitant to take a ship up into their facility that had only been lifted out of the water once in over thirty years. They had heard many negative rumors about the condition of the bottom of this ship and told us they couldn't afford for the metal to collapse while it was in dry dock. The ship could fall and disable their facility.

They insisted on bringing over divers and sending them down to inspect the bottom. They had heard that a survey conducted by Lockheed detected large dents and several fractures and cracks, indicating that the bottom plates would have to be replaced. We realized that the report said the ship was bad, but we had faith that God wouldn't give us a ship with a bad bottom and leave us here to work on it for four years.

Divers showed up at Pier 66, donned their wet suits and diving gear and down they went. We anxiously waited on the docks. Although having heard about that bad report for more than four years, we still refused to believe it. One way or the other, we knew the bottom would have to be okay.

The divers surfaced and reported that there was so much growth on the bottom that it was difficult to give an accurate appraisal. But they did see what appeared to be three large indentations and said, "The stabilizer fins are so rusty you could stick your arm right through them." Everything seemed to agree with the Lockheed report made twelve years earlier.

These were professional ship surveyors, licensed men with integrity, men with strong backgrounds and years of experience. Now, we had more than one bad report, this one describing the exact damage they had seen. The shipyard executives approached us and said they had decided that they were willing to take the ship up if we still wanted to go ahead. "We think she's a sound ship," we said. "Please take the ship up. We believe she has a good bottom."

We called our friends at Crowley Maritime and asked them to tow Spirit to dry dock. They said yes, then called their competitor Foss Tow. The two companies donated one towboat each to take us to the shipyard in their very first joint venture.

A few days later, the Spirit was taken up into the drydock at Unimar Shipyard and the results of the "out of the water inspection" were shocking! The stabilizer fins were fine, about the same thickness as when they had been applied brand new. The propeller, rudder and shaft had not been repaired or maintained in thirty years, and except for a multitude of marine creatures attached to every single inch of them, they were in excellent condition. The shipyard foreman told us that the chances of that happening were almost nil.

We scraped away the marine growth and searched for the dents. But, amazingly, there were no dents, no cracks, no fractures. The metal was smooth, like a baby's cheek.

Were the dents ever there? There was no indication that they ever had been, yet at least two professional survey teams reported damage as fact. Except for replacing some welds, Spirit's bottom was the best in her class.

We cleaned, sandblasted and repainted her bottom, painted the top side, welded some metal seams, cleaned up the shaft, attached zincs, checked the sea chests and dropped the Spirit back into the water, her bottom ready for sea.

One company after another donated major marine equipment: a water maker to convert sea water to fresh from Beaird Corporation; an oily-water separator for our waste oil from

Separation and Recovery Systems; a Humphrey marine sanitation device from Byrne, Rice and Turner; zincs from Belmont Metals; fenders from Seaward International; radio equipment from Hull Electronics, Regency Electronics and Pioneer Marketing; bridge electronics from Gemini Marine; repair services from Sperry; parts from Hatch and Kirk; two emergency radio beacon instruments from A.C.R.; an air horn from Kahlenberg Brothers; a shore-boat wheel from Johnson Propeller; a Loran C and a huge discount on a state-of-the-art Global Points Navigation System from Raytheon—along with countless other valuable donations.

We took Spirit to our port berth and finished repairs. I knew that within weeks, the dream would be a reality. Spirit would be ready to load cargo and sail.

Then, one day in prayer, I felt the Lord say, "Son, what is it of me that you want?" The question came with such power and authority that I thought I needed to blurt out an immediate response. What did I want?

I wasn't prepared for such a question. Then I remembered that Solomon was asked such a question as this. I'd better not be a fool and answer without great thought. But I said, "Lord, I don't have to think about it. I know. Lord, I know that this is going to sound like bold talk. I want to be Your steward. You must have many others, but I want to be one of them.

"There are books about how to be a steward for God, but that's not the kind of steward I mean, God. Not a steward over things that You give me, I want to be steward over the things that belong to the kingdom, that belong to You, that are held in preparation for the great revival—things that will march on cities and run on the walls, that will fill ships for spiritual revolution in distant lands, that will feed children and hungry people, that will clothe the naked—your stores, God, the things You want to give away. I realize that the things in Your warehouses are not for storing up but for giving out.

"You are not a 'collecting God', You are a giving God. Show me Lord, tell me, teach me, give me divine direction and understanding, to operate the real storehouse, the one that stores the property of God Almighty Himself.

After that, God gave me two dreams. Never have I had dreams so real. In the first, I was standing in an arid wasteland. I saw a few men hoeing and tending a wheat field, trying to prepare for sowing a thirsty harsh land. I was standing beside a large cement well, which towered a few feet over my head. I heard a rumbling in the belly of the earth, and water began to come out of the well. I stood back and saw myself in the shape of a large, round PVC pipe, very white and very empty. Water poured inside my PVC pipe and down the slope through a smaller pipe and into other feeders that brought moisture to the field where the men were working.

The workmen were full of joy as the water penetrated the dry harsh soil. As the water continued to flow through me, the flow increased. Looking out, I saw more feeder pipes and new fields springing up. I began to behold fields as far as I could see. More and more pipe, more and more workmen, more and more fields. The water continued to increase its flow. There was a roar and a rumbling like I'd never heard, the sound deafening like a locomotive train engine beside my head. The ground shook with the volume and massive flow of the water.

Suddenly, I was gripped with fear. I thought, *I'd better hold back some of this water. Look at the thousands of workmen that are depending on me and my water. I better hold a reserve for later when it will be needed.*

I squeezed off the flow and, as I did, the fields began to dry up. The workmen in the far distance watched as their fields became dry and withered. They picked up their tools and walked off.

I was heartbroken and spoke to the well, "Forgive me, I'm operating in fear, not by your power." I released the water and again the fields sprang up, green and clean. The workers returned in great joy. The well continued, unending, unstoppable. Suddenly, I understood more about God.

In the second dream, the mighty ship Spirit was in the harbor of a desert land that was parched and dry, somewhere in East Africa. We had fifteen military flat bed trucks which had all been off-loaded. The trucks were parked a couple of hundred yards from a wired compound of refugees. Hot and tired, I sat on the running board fender of the lead truck listening to the joy, laughter, praise and song in the compound. The people were happy because of the food, milk and medicines the Lord had brought them.

As I looked across the barren ground between the camp and the trucks, three men approached me. I saw two black men dressed with white medical coats and one tall blonde man in the middle.

As they came closer, I noticed that the man in the middle was a Christian singer. I thought, *How strange, what would he be doing in a place like this?* But I identified him as a man of God and this was significant. Not who he was but what he was.

I didn't recognize the other two men, and the singer didn't know me. He approached and said, "Excuse me, is the boss around?"

I said facetiously, "Not now, but can I help you in the meantime?"

"We need one of these trucks to load up supplies from here and drive to a distant compound where there are starving people."

I immediately evaluated the circumstances. Within the hour, the trucks were due to return to the harbor to be reloaded aboard the ship Spirit and then sail onto its next assignment. If I released a truck, I knew I would never see it again.

I handed the singer the keys and told him it was full of fuel and ready to go. As I started to walk off, I turned back and said to him, "If another man of God asks you for the use of this vehicle, don't you deny him."

I awoke and analyzed the two dreams. In the first, I was the receiving pipe, receiving the precious life-giving water and channeling it through the small pipes to the laborers in the field. Some were seeding, some were plowing and some were harvesting—as long as I hoarded nothing, remaining clean inside and prepared to receive the water's flow. But I realized that my will and my actions could stifle the flow of water. If I were willing to stay open, the water could flow at a mighty volume, ever increasing. I understood that it wasn't receiving from God but releasing what God gave me that was the true value of a real steward. But it wouldn't operate in fear. It must remain bold and open to the water God would supply.

The second dream took a little more thought. The singer and his two companions had approached me. I hadn't known the other men, but the singer stood tall in my mind as a man who loved God.

He was not significant other than his spiritual identification. The request for the truck was godly and served a righteous purpose, and I realized I wouldn't see the truck again. But the truck belonged to God, not to me. The use of the truck and the task at hand had been completed.

The Lord was teaching me this phase of the theory, greater need first. So as I released the truck, I wasn't to take thought of it again. God was the great supplier. I could accomplish the next job with the remaining fourteen trucks, and God would reward me with more any time He wanted to.

But my warning to the singer was to keep the chain going, **greater need first**. If another righteous man of God had a greater need at the end of his accomplishment, he was also to release. And in this way, the blessings flowed and the chain would grow.

I understand your concept, God, and so I pledge my service.

15

JUST WAITING FOR US

Our final hours in Seattle were strenuous. We worked eighteen to twenty-hour days, battling snow and ice in order to finish last minute repairs, bring aboard a spare anchor and load up available steel and equipment we knew we would need for future repairs.

One of our last evenings in town, some of our crew found time to attend a church service. A man there had a vision in which he saw the Spirit moving through the water, but gliding above it, the propeller not turning. The man said that the ship was moving not by her own power but by the "Spirit" of the Lord.

Before sailing from Seattle, we wrote letters to certain authorities requesting permission for Spirit to come into the Port of L.A. at a reduced rate. We had been told that two other not-for-profit ships were denied the same request but, nevertheless, we wrote and we prayed.

On February 18, two Crowley tugs came to escort us from the bay. We radioed the Coast Guard—Spirit was going on a sea trial. Tugs tied a line onto us. Only four faithful friends stood by on the dock to cast off.

We slowly pulled out, saying good-bye to the city that had been our host for four years and five months. It was a moment in history we would never forget as Captain George Folden gave the tugs a final order to let loose their ropes.

Our hearts pounded with excitement as the tug lines released and the Spirit ship moved through the Puget Sound, away from her escorts, alone and under her own power for the first time in thirty-four years. Words cannot describe our great joy!

As the ship moved effortlessly through the water, Sondra and I stood on the flying bridge, holding each other and praising God for this great miracle He had wrought. It was the manifestation of a beautiful dream! Our hearts were filled with overflowing love for our Creator and gratitude to Him for the things He had allowed us to see. The forty-six year-old ship—that expert after expert said would never again sail—was soaring through the Puget Sound and out to the Pacific Ocean!

The eight-day sail down the U.S. West Coast was anything but uneventful. We sailed the Straits of Juan de Fuega, dropped anchor in Devil's Cove and finished some stow work. Two days later we weighed anchor and radioed the Coast Guard that the Spirit's sea trial was a success and that we were going out to sea.

As the ship sailed from Puget Sound, the sizable waves we met caused the Spirit's bow to rise and fall. Many of the crew stood talking together on deck atop the hatch covers. Then, as abruptly as if a hand grenade had been tossed into their midst, the group scattered toward the rails in all directions, painfully experiencing their first dose of seasickness. As the storm continued, few of us escaped the dreadful nausea. That night, while the chief engineer concentrated his efforts on the ship's stack, the most experienced junior members of our engine crew remained sick in their cabins, while others took their place.

When the main engine showed definite signs of overheating, the "engineers" faithfully recorded the soaring temperature but did nothing to alleviate the problem. Sometime about midnight, sixty miles off the coast, suddenly and unexpectedly, there was an explosion in a piston of the ship's main engine. The bridge kicked on the fire alarms and each member of the crew bolted from their rooms and scurried down the narrow passageways. Smoke wafting up from the engine room, while the ship pitched in the night, created an eerie feeling as the crew made their way through the dark corridors.

I stood at the life jacket station pitching flotation vests to each one on their way to their muster area on deck. Would we be forced to kick over the rafts and leap into the frigid black water of the Pacific Ocean?

It wasn't a pleasant thought and the situation was tense. But we were blessed to be under the command of George Folden, a highly qualified master, as well as Walt Carruthers, a chief engineer with years of experience. With the captain's professional calm manner and a few well-placed jokes from Walt, our tension quickly broke and, by a few hours later, the engineers had completed a temporary fix for the problem. We continued on our journey to Los Angeles. The remainder of the trip was beautiful and uneventful. The ship ran like a dream.

When we arrived in Los Angeles, we requested permission from the pilots to anchor as close as possible to our warehouse, hoping we would receive a berth at the same pier. We launched our twenty-six foot personnel boat, and Sondra and I went ashore to find out the results of our requests for dockage. We were thrilled to discover that the Port of Los Angeles had agreed to welcome us into port for a reduced fee of $.04 a square foot or about $600 a month. The only berth they had available was Berth 60 in San Pedro, the very one we requested, only a few hundred yards from our warehouse.

Finally, it was time to make a decision. I asked the Lord where He wanted us to sail on the Spirit's first mission, thinking He would put on my heart a certain nation, a specific port or route, a mission that He had ordained. Instead He said, to my surprise, "Wherever you go, I'll be there waiting." We decided to go to Nicaragua, El Salvador and Guatemala. Fire one—our first official mercy trip.

An interesting turn of events took place during Spirit's eight-day sail from Seattle to Los Angeles. The communist government of Nicaragua held free elections and, to everyone's great surprise, a landslide victory was won by a Democratic presidential candidate. We had long wanted to make this Central American country one of our first ports of call, but private U.S. humanitarian assistance to that nation had been complicated, if not impossible. Now, because of the elections, by the time we were set to sail from Los Angeles, Nicaragua would be free!

We teamed up with a Central American organization named Verbo Christian Ministries. Verbo operates churches, schools, hospitals, dental clinics and orphanages in all three of our target countries, as well as in several others. We agreed to work as supplier and shipper. Verbo would serve as foreign coordinator and receiver/distributor.

Sondra and I flew to Central America in order to meet with Verbo personnel. We felt confident about this capable, responsible and godly organization being the recipients of Spirit's first load of supplies.

But how disappointed we were upon our first meeting with the Director of Customs in Guatemala. Two Verbo elders, Sondra and I attended the meeting with great anticipation, thinking surely the government would be anxious to receive help for their people. But the customs official promptly and unabashedly explained to us, in the presence of several witnesses, that in order to import charitable goods to the country of Guatemala, one must allow customs officials to take their pick of the supplies, and whatever was left over could then be received by orphans and others. She even launched into a detailed example, just to be certain that we understood her.

Later, however, we were introduced to a man who was head of the government department that supervised customs. He was a new Christian and arranged for all of our cargo to make entry intact and free of charge. A private stevedore company offered longshoremen without charge, and the railroad committed to providing boxcars to move the supplies to Guatemala City.

In our meeting with El Salvador's Vice Minister of the Interior, he promised to see that all government fees would be waived, including customs. But, he warned us that the Port authorities were autonomous and difficult. They had never waived fees, even for government humanitarian aid, and he was quite certain that they would not cooperate with us.

Later that day, we met with the port representative, who was, as it turned out, a Christian man who saw this as an opportunity to help his country. He readily agreed to waive the port fees, even offering to provide longshoremen without charge. But, not knowing that God had already cleared the way with the government, he warned us that the El Salvadoran authorities would never agree to waive their portion of the charges!

In Los Angeles, the crew continued to prepare the Spirit for her voyage. But where were we going to get 4,000 tons of good quality relief items? That was an enormous amount of food, clothing and medical supplies. Even our full warehouse held only about one third of what the Spirit could carry.

The Lord gave us a peace about it and, before long, World Opportunities International joined forces with us and sent truckload after truckload of top-quality medical equipment, supplies and food. Tim, who owned Yesterday's Silk-Screening Company (and who had so generously shared his warehouse with us) contributed 15,000 brand-new printed shirts to use as crew uniforms and gifts for the poor. The Los Angeles Unified School District donated thousands of student desks. Nissin Foods gave hundreds of thousands of packages of dehydrated soup. A.D.R.A. contributed tons of washed, pressed, fumigated and baled top-quality clothing. Reap International donated thousands of dollars worth of medical equipment and supplies.

During this period of loading, Loren, who was paying for our warehouse, asked me to pray for an 18% increase in his business. He said that if he had an 18% increase, he would double our warehouse space.

We desperately needed more warehouse space so I began to pray for a 50% increase for Loren and asked the crew to do the same. It wasn't long before we heard that Loren's business had shown a 50% increase in the first few months of that year. It was incredible! I rejoiced, knowing that my prayers had been answered and feeling that God had raised up a champion for us in Loren. I began to plan for our new warehouse.

About this time, Loren stopped by to tell me that indeed business was booming, so much so that he had decided to purchase a new warehouse instead of leasing! Unfortunately, this purchase would leave him short of cash so he had to cut off our support. *Rats,* I thought, *I prayed myself right out of a blessing.*

But in April, the Port of Los Angeles called to say the Maritime Affairs Committee had decided to cancel our rent. "Cancel our rent?" we said, alarmed. "Does this mean we have to leave?"

"No, no," the port official said. "We are canceling your rent. You can stay but you don't need to pay rent anymore. In fact, we are going to return all the rent you've paid. We'll be mailing you a check for $23,000."

This was incredible! We had never asked for this consideration, never even thought it possible. But had the port not made their decision to sponsor us, the news of Loren's situation would have been devastating. Instead, I realized that the Lord was teaching me a lesson. He had chosen to use Loren to help us—and He was blessing Loren—but Loren had not been our source.

We moved the tugboat to Los Angeles from San Francisco in order to house the warehouse and office crew. Only one of her two main engines was operational, and we had chosen a poor time of the year to sail. Seas were huge just outside of the bay, the waves washing over the back deck. We tossed and turned like we were no bigger than a freckle, but we finally showed up in Los Angeles days later—tired but no worse for wear.

We continued to work hard at preparing the ship for sea and loading cargo. We got truckload after truckload of those school desks from the Los Angeles Unified School District. The desks were awkward to load and took up an immense amount of space; they wouldn't stack. They just kind of piled and, on more than one occasion, I seriously wondered if we should be taking them to Nicaragua.

Another day, our driver backed the truck down the dock and threw up the door. It was stacked to the very back, full from top to bottom with thousands of gallons of hydraulic oil. "Hydraulic oil?" I asked. "Take that back. We need food for the Nicaraguans."

"Oh, please," the driver said. "The company was so blessed to give us this."

I said, "No. Take it back. Get rid of this oil. I'm only taking food. Get rid of it."

The driver continued to plead his case. "It would be so embarrassing to return this load. Can't we just take this one truckload?"

"Okay," I agreed. "One truckload. But now go and concentrate on food."

By the time we were ready to sail, we had loaded food, new and used clothing, medical supplies, hospital furniture, medical machines, dental equipment, vitamins, medicine, seeds, buckets, tools, crop sprayers, building supplies, school supplies, office equipment, Bible literature and Bibles, paint, household items, three vans, one truck, thousands of school desks and a big load of hydraulic oil.

We were ready to sail by August.

16

FROM JESUS WITH LOVE

Exactly 1,774 days after taking ownership, the "Good Ship Spirit" set sail on her first mission of mercy. On Sunday afternoon, August 12, at 1:35 in the afternoon, a Los Angeles harbor pilot boarded as two Crowley Maritime tugs pulled alongside to escort Spirit through Angels Gate out to sea. She now steamed on her own, bound for Corinto, Nicaragua.

The last days before we sailed had been filled with difficult decisions. The final word from our Verbo contact in Managua was that port authorities and longshoremen in Corinto were going to charge the ship $85,000 to berth and off-load cargo, even if we did not employ the Nicaraguan longshoremen and unloaded the holds with our own labor.

The men in charge of the port and longshoremen were Sandinistas, and they were not interested in any benefit that the new government, their country, or the poor might receive from our donations. When the Verbo coordinator in Corinto told them of the sacrifice and the thousands of volunteers involved in bringing these donated supplies to the people of Nicaragua, and of the children and elderly who would receive the benefit of the much-needed food, clothing and medical items, the supervisor responded, "Don't get sentimental on me. I know all North Americans have money. The charge is $85,000!"

We did not have $85,000 and, according to international maritime law, once a ship accrues expenses beyond its ability to pay, the ship may be attached and held until the fee is paid. Also, from the time the ship is attached, additional port expenses accumulate. It is not unusual for fees of several thousand dollars a day to be added on to the original debt. What happens in most cases is that the vessel is seized by the port and then the officials are able to do whatever they want with it.

After five long years of work, even the mere thought of losing the Spirit at the first port of call was devastating, but we kept quiet about all of this and, along with Jamie, prayed about what we should do. We felt confident that God was sending us to Nicaragua and we were determined to sail.

It was a beautiful voyage. The days at sea were calm but interesting as each day took on a character all its own. We saw whales, sea turtles and birds of many types. Dolphins rode the waves at Spirit's bow. As the crew cheered, one dolphin (almost like an escapee from Sea World) performed back flips along the length of the hull. The evening brought breathtaking sunsets, silent light-storms on the horizon, and warm, balmy breezes. The waves were with us, the wind was with us and the currents were with us. Most exciting of all, the Lord was with us!

Even so, the trip was not without trials. Temperatures soared around the tip of Ensenada. The men in the engine room and those in construction on deck, dressed in welding gear, endured 130 degree heat. The ice machine could not make enough ice to keep us cool, and for a few days it was unbearably hot.

During the first twelve days at sea we experienced little outside communication and not much word from home. Then, two days before reaching Nicaraguan waters, we got word via radio transmission that the men who controlled the port of Corinto had been fired and replaced. Newly-elected President Violetta de Chomorro had written a letter to the port notifying them that all port fees we had previously been informed of would now be waived!

When the Spirit sailed into the harbor, the Nicaraguan government and port authorities rolled out the red carpet.

Men from the army came and offered to provide trucks and

"Spirit" in action. Forty feet longer than a football field, seven stories high. In Port-au-Prince, Haiti with the U.S. invasion fleet. (bottom)

U.S. Coast Guard Photo By: Robin Ressler

security assistance as well as anything else they might be able to do. But, in strictest confidence, they told us that although they—the army—were willing to help us, we had to watch out for navy guys, because "they would want to take everything for themselves." They then said they'd place a guard at the gangway to protect us from navy personnel.

Soon afterwards, navy officers arrived. They told us how proud they were that we were in their harbor and that they would assist us in any capacity. But, in strictest confidence, the Navy told us that we had to watch out for those army guys because *they* would take everything for themselves. They offered to help us by placing a guard on the gangway to prevent the army from coming aboard and taking whatever they want.

It was quite amusing. There was God's great ship, the Spirit, docked in Corinto with a royal guard at her gangway, and two armed military men—one navy, one army—keeping a watchful eye on one another and anyone else that might attempt to take things from us.

Nicaraguan port officials came aboard and told us they were waiving all fees and thought they could get volunteers to come unload our ship and work for free. They would ask the union and see.

Later they came back to tell us that there were so many volunteers, they had to rotate them in shifts. Professional stevedores came to work their difficult and dangerous job. We were surprised to see they had no hard hats or gloves, and some were even without shoes. The men worked for hours and hours without rest.

Food was very scarce during this time in Nicaragua, so we were blessed to be able to serve the stevedores giant hamburgers, ice cream and all sorts of other wonderful food.

When the port officials paid us a visit, we asked, "Is there anything that we can do for you here at the port, something the Spirit crew can do to say 'thank you' for all you are doing for us?"

The officials replied, "Thank you, but our problem is not only food. You see, all of our cranes, forklifts and power equipment are down and not running. We've run out of hydraulic fluid and no more is available, so everything for us has come to a stop."

"Gentlemen," we said, amazed, "the Lord has a very special gift for you. It just so happens we have a full truckload of brand new hydraulic fluid." The lesson was obvious.

While we were very busy off-loading cargo, the Nicaraguan President, Violetta Chomorro, graciously invited the crew to the palace for a lunch and reception to thank us for what we were doing. The crew was working an incredible amount of hours, almost round the clock, to accomplish the job of feeding children in need, so they were not able to attend. But Sondra and I decided that we should personally go to thank the President for her help. We informed her staff of the situation and suggested that perhaps the whole crew might be able to come another time, after we had finished the task. It would be only Sondra and me attending from among our crew this time.

We made our way to the palace and were brought into a large reception area which was set up for a sizable party, along with news cameras and all the gear for interviews. We arrived with only Carlos, the head of Verbo Ministries, Bob and Myra, the local Verbo missionaries, and Cesar, the Nicaraguan Consul General to the U.S. Our number was far from the large party obviously expected.

When the President's staff saw the small size of our group, a flurry of activity and frantic conversation began. Sondra and I couldn't understand the Spanish language and didn't know what the problem was. Carlos, who speaks the language fluently, leaned over to me and said softly, "It seems that no one had told the President that our crew declined the invitation." Apparently they were afraid to pass this information on—for some reason we didn't understand. Carlos wrinkled his face and said, "I think we're in a lot of trouble. It would appear that the President is not too happy."

There was more frantic activity and loud conversation. This continued for almost an hour.

Finally, someone appeared on the President's balcony, which was adjacent to her private office, and spoke to us. Carlos wrinkled his face once again and translated. It seemed that the lunch and party had been reduced to five minutes with the President in her office.

Because of this unfortunate misunderstanding, I expected the President to be curt and withdrawn—she was anything but. She was gracious and lovely, yet very presidential and official. We sat in a small circle around her large chair. She sat rigid with a strong posture, but she was charming nonetheless, with a regal, almost Queen Elizabeth presence.

She greeted us politely and thanked us for what we had been doing to help her people. Then she stated that she had scheduled radio and television interviews and that the newspaper and camera men would be photographing this session. Almost as if choreographed, the doors opened and news people began to enter. As they took their positions, I leaned forward. "President Chomorro, please permit me to explain. We don't give interviews to the press."

She stiffened. Her focus narrowed as she looked into my eyes. I could see I had further offended her and was in deep water with no way out except to say it all.

"President, if I could explain. We've heard of the trouble in your country and that the food supply was short, medicine shelves nearly empty and the hospitals and clinics had practically nothing to work with. In the short couple of days we've been here, we've seen that it's far worse than reported. We've come with thousands of tons of baby food, rice, beans, flour, dehydrated food, medical supplies, clothes, building materials and much, much more. We have come with the love of Christ to give freely to your people at no charge.

"Please, Mrs. President, hear our hearts. We have come to

love you and your people, with the love of God. We have no interest in interviews, reporters or television. We come quietly to help your people in their time of need. We haven't come to take pictures of your children in their poverty and hunger to take back to sell for so much a month to Americans. Neither have we come for photos and interviews with the elderly or impoverished. We don't want your people to think that rich Americans are the answer to their problem. We want them to know the truth—that God has heard the cry of the orphans, widows, elderly and poor.

"Here in Managua is Casa Bernabe, an orphanage of 140 children who have been fasting for one day every week, praying for our safe arrival. This orphanage is reported to be your country's best, but it has no windows or doors—only dirt floors. They have little medical attention; food is sparse and they have little to wear. We'll be giving food and supplies to this orphanage (which is run by the local church) for them to distribute. We would like to remain behind the scenes so that the Nicaraguan people will see the local church meeting the needs of the city's poor. Then they will know that it was God who heard their cry."

President Chomorro began to smile and relax. She sat back deeply in her chair and with a wave of her left hand, said, "Take the reporters all out, all of them." As quickly as they had entered, they disappeared.

The great love the President had for her people began to flow out of her as she talked. She told us of their needs and of her dream for her nation. She thanked us for respecting their dignity.

We saw the depth of her character as she told us how, when the people wrote her letters, she stayed up late each night, reading every one. Like a grandmother doting over her grandchildren— each child so precious to her—she longed to meet their needs.

The President shared with us, "This very day I toured some of Managua's public schools and was grieved to see thousands of children sitting on the dirt without paper, pencils or even desks. Those few who were fortunate enough to have a desk carried it for miles each day to and from their home, balanced atop their heads, just to be certain it wouldn't be stolen." She leaned back in her chair and sighed. "If only you'd been able to bring school desks."

Can you imagine the excitement we felt as we told her, "We have thousands of desks stuffed in our cargo holds." We realized then that the Lord had orchestrated our **whole** load!

We had been in her office for a very long time; it seemed like hours. Afraid we were overstaying our welcome, I then made my third protocol blunder. I stood up and told the President we would be leaving now because we knew she was busy. A startled look came over Mrs. Chomorro's face as she stood to her feet. Apparently, proper protocol dictates that it is the President's place to stand and determine the timing for each meeting's end. She looked at me. Then she with a soft chuckle and we with our relieved smiles, said our warm good-byes. Before we walked out very far, she called us back into the office and asked more questions about Casa Bernabe. She also gave us signed photos of herself, which we highly cherish.

We left knowing that we had entered a completely different space with the President, not one of politics and protocol, but one of genuine personal friendship. It was a relationship that has stood fast, her office extending invitations for dinners and receptions in America. And during times since, when disaster has plagued her country, President Chomorro has reached out to us for assistance.

❖❖❖

Once, after a rare tsunami hit Nicaragua, drowning large groups of people and destroying whole villages, we were contacted by the U.S. Pentagon. A colonel called to say that a request had come through the White House to the Pentagon. They would be providing a C5 Galaxy, our largest military cargo plane, for trips into the disaster area on the Nicaraguan Pacific Coast. There had been a request from the Nicaraguan President, he said, to the U.S. President for emergency aid. The colonel went on to say that our participation was specifically requested by Mrs.

Students carry their school desks to and from their homes

Crew prays hand in hand with Nicaraguan longshoremen

اتي اسوع المسيح المحبة

DE JESUS CHRISTO CON AMOR

FROM JESUS WITH LOVE

DA GESU CON AMORE

MIT LIEBE VON JESUS

DE JESUS AVEC AMOUR

ОТ ИИСУСА С ЛЮБОВЬЮ

從耶穌的慈愛而來

This is the "Friend Ships" label that is attached to the cargo of international shipments. It reads "From Jesus With Love" in Arabic, Spanish, English, Italian, German, French, Russian and Chinese.

C5 Galaxy full of food, medical supplies and clothes to Nicaragua

Chomorro for a joint effort with the U.S. military in a humanitarian airlift. The colonel asked if we could provide food and other emergency relief. We agreed. For us, this was the beginning of many airlifts.

A few weeks later, we received a copy of a State Department newsletter which circulates in Washington D.C. In this paper was a story about our charity. The heading read, "Who are these Quiet Giants of the West?" I felt like shouting back, "Jesus and Company!"

❖❖❖

Just before two o'clock in the morning, we finished off-loading in Nicaragua, our first port of call. A difficult job, one that we had thought would take at least three weeks, was completed in just three days as God blessed us beyond our wildest expectations. As we thanked Him for the way each battle we had faced had been fought for us in advance, we realized that the red carpet on which we had been walking was a result of those 140 orphans and their sweet petitions to the Lord.

The Spirit sailed on to El Salvador, delivering medical supplies, and then to Guatemala, discharging a variety of goods, including equipment that Verbo would use to establish a hospital in Guatemala City for the benefit of the poor.

Spirit returned to Los Angeles and quickly began to be reloaded for a second mission to Central America. Having seen the needs firsthand, we felt that this time we would load almost exclusively for Nicaragua with a smaller load for Guatemala. We set the end of February as a sail date.

Our main office consisted of a 20 foot trailer in the warehouse (cramped quarters with no privacy). Our operations were growing by leaps and bounds, and we felt that we needed a larger, more secure and professional spot from which to work.

An office owned by the port, located directly across the street from our warehouse, had remained available for several months and, although we had discussed the space many times, we hadn't had the courage to take on a new financial responsibility. Now we were beginning to feel as if we should take it. Finally, we decided to do it. The day after we made the decision, a friend called to say that he would pay the monthly rent. All that we had to come up with was a two month deposit.

That day's mail brought an unexpected check for almost the exact amount we needed for the deposit. We couldn't help but notice that the check had been written a week earlier, but had not been mailed until the day we had made a definite decision—in faith—to take the office space.

All the office furniture and equipment we needed was stored right in our own warehouse, so we moved in and stretched our legs.

Although we had almost enough fuel for the second voyage, it was going to be close. Then out of the blue, two movie companies in a row asked to shoot footage at the Spirit, delaying our work only slightly and bringing in some $12,000 worth of "site" fees, which provided the funds we needed to purchase enough fuel to complete the mission.

This time the ship was loaded with tons of building materials. There was over a million dollars worth of Peachtree and Anderson frames and windows. They were gas filled, double paned, tempered, tinted, roll out and half windows—some of the best available! There were doors and screen doors, hundreds of ceiling tiles, thousands of square feet of carpeting and several thousand gallons of paint. These materials would be used to help construct and repair churches, clinics, hospitals, orphanages and schools. We collected truckloads of school desks for the children and a massive amount of dry goods, including hundreds of thousands of servings of Nissin soup.

A nurse named Charley contacted us. It seemed that during a medical mission to Puerto Cabezas, on the east coast of Nicaragua, Charley got a glimpse of the (very) decrepit building that housed the village orphans. So she talked to her friend Harry, a British tea shop owner from Santa Monica. Harry talked to his wife, Jan, and together they talked to their friends Bud and Bob and Derek.

Before long, this capable group had acquired an entire brand new, ready-to-erect orphanage, including walls, doors, ceiling, foundation, sinks, showers, toilets, a well and even pots and pans. Charley, Harry and friends had no idea how they would get this building to Nicaragua, but then they heard about the Spirit and delivered it to our dock. We joyfully loaded it, setting the huge roof trusses on top of the center hatch cover as we prepared to sail.

In February, we once again set out for Nicaragua, school desks piled high on the decks. And, once again, we were greeted with open arms. We discharged the cargo and moved it by truck to Managua for distribution. But we soon learned that the orphanage could not be moved by truck to its destination of Puerto Cabezas on the Atlantic Coast because some Contra-turned-bandits, with high-tech rocket launchers and automatic weapons, were robbing trucks on the highway.

In Puerto Cabezas, we saw wounded drivers—shot while transiting the road—being carried into the hospital. Obviously, an airlift was the answer. The kind of plane necessary would be something like a C130 Hercules, a large military flying warehouse that lifts 30,000 pounds of cargo, has a huge door that opens in the rear of the plane, big balloon tires, tremendous power and great wingspan, capable of short takeoffs and landings so that it can set down in fields, small strips and dirt roads. Just the ticket. And we knew where to find one.

We talked to "LeSea Global", which had just acquired a C130 but had not flown it anywhere yet. We asked them how they would like to take their maiden voyage helping a group of Nicaraguan orphans in Puerto Cabezas. It turns out that they were looking for just such a test run to train their flight and cargo engineers. Without hesitation or price, the C130 was in the air, flying toward Nicaragua.

What a sight to see the beautiful plane come in for a landing

Delivering a complete, ready to erect orphanage to Puerto Cabazas, Nicaragua by ship and C130 aircraft.

in Managua! We picked up the orphanage, piece by piece, flew it at 18,000 feet over the bandits' heads, and dropped down toward the little village of Puerto Cabezas. We landed, made a hard right turn down an old dirt road, and headed for the square at the edge of town. People gathered around the plane by the hundreds. Schools let the children out to meet us. Everyone was excited.

We discharged the building materials. Charley's British tea shop team—who had used up their vacations away from their families to pound nails in the hot tropical sun—was erecting the structure. They would yell at us as we took off in the Hercules to collect another load, "More nails, Mate!" or "Another hammer!" Each time, we sped up the engines and navigated back down the dirt road leading out of town. Forty-five minutes later, we would be sitting on the runway in Managua where a group of Verbo crew were waiting to reload. We made six flights over two days, supplying the village with food, clothing and medical supplies.

On one run to the coast, as the C130 came heading up the dirt road leading into town, the airplane crew said they wanted to test how quickly they could discharge a load of food and clothes. When we reached the square, we dropped the big rear door to the airplane, shut down the two engines on the left side and sped up the outside engines on the right side as we applied the inside wheel brakes. This big four-engine, three-story airplane sat in the middle of the town square, spinning around like a top. We unlatched the pallets one at a time as the plane spit them out in a wide circle.

We discharged the entire load in just about three minutes. As she came around for the last spin, we sped up the inside engines, took off down the dirt road and flew back to Managua, all without one stop. The C130 pilots never had so much fun!

On our last flight to Puerto Cabezas, we said good-bye to the work team, shook hands with the locals, threw candy to the kids and prepared to leave. Harry, one of the "Brits" who were building the orphanage, said to the pilot, "Listen, mate, if you would like to do a little fly-by, I have a Sony 8mm video camera.

I'll take a pretty picture and send it to you." The captain looked at him with a smile and a wink, saying, "Sure thing, Mate. I'll do a nice little fly-by." I thought, *Uh-oh. This sounds like trouble.*

As we took off down the old dirt road out of town and lifted into the air, we took a hard right bank and flew six miles over the snow-white beach and the transparent, turquoise-blue Caribbean Sea. We banked back another hard right and headed straight toward the village as the engines roared. I knew we were at full throttle, skimming the water like an attack bomber, sneaking up on its target. The pilot lifted up the plane just as we made our approach to the village, but still we were only at treetop level. The local houses were built on stilts with cheap, wood siding, grass and tin roofs. These were not the kind of buildings that would withstand much low level flight. I looked out the side window and saw some old tin roofs shaking and lifting from the wind of the propellers and thought, *We're going to blow the town over and have to come back and rebuild the whole thing!*

Out of the cockpit, I heard a crewmen holler, "There, there it is. Two o'clock, to your right."

"I see it! I see it!" said the pilot as he made the adjustment.

Harry stood atop the two-story frame orphanage. Everything happened in a matter of seconds, but as we closed in, I could see him looking frantically from side to side. Being a pilot himself, Harry was certain that the vortex wind from the four propellers of the low-flying plane was going to blow over the orphanage that he had been working on so diligently for a solid week. As we made the pass over the building, Harry and the C130 pilot were nearly eye to eye! Harry threw his camera one way and jumped in the other direction, into the distant sand below. The C130 airplane then put her nose into the air and headed back to America.

Harry wasn't hurt at all, and even the building was okay, but it was a long week of wondering and waiting before hearing a report. Nevertheless, we had a great time, exciting and full of adventure.

17

HEARTS FOR RUSSIA

After our second mission to Nicaragua, the ship sailed on to Guatemala. As she headed back to Los Angeles, I sent word from the main office to announce the destination of the Spirit's next voyage.

Up to this time, the Spirit had sailed just off the coast of the Americas, delivering to our not-too-distant neighbors. But the next trip would be different, very different. Instead of a fourteen-day sail in the Pacific, this would be a forty-five day, transatlantic mission—destination U.S.S.R. We had no fuel, no load and we knew no one in the Soviet Union, but the crew received their marching orders with excitement.

We got word that food shortages were on the rise in Russia and throughout the territory of the U.S.S.R. A serious situation—it was said—was on the horizon.

We began to gather food at the warehouse in San Pedro. We searched for missions and ministries that were interested in being partners with us on this trip, but, in the spring of 1991, we could find very few people with a heart to help the Soviet Union .

We met with the leaders of some church groups who told us they feared this trip was too far and too much of an unknown. Perhaps if we went somewhere safer and closer to home, it would be of more interest to them. But we felt this was where God was sending us.

The Spirit returned home on April 26, and, by this time, LeSea Global decided they would like to be partners with us on the next mission.

The time element was critical, and we struggled to determine the best schedule. We knew it was possible for the port of Leningrad to ice up in the winter, so we needed to move quickly, setting July 1 as a sail date. That left only eight weeks to load for the Soviet Union. It had taken sixteen weeks to procure, organize, load cargo and prepare the ship for previous trips, so we knew it would take a miracle in order for us to sail by July 1. I spoke to the crew; they were charged up and ready to go, willing to put in the extra hours and work Sundays, if necessary, and to proceed with the intense commitment it would take to make this happen.

Few people seemed interested in lending a hand to help what was then, still, Communist U.S.S.R. A notable exception was World Opportunities International, which has always stood by us in everything we've done. Most other groups were negative or completely disinterested, as it was yet to be fashionable to go to Russia. It seemed we were just slightly ahead of our time.

We continued to collect our normal, incoming food, medical supplies and seed. We loaded tons of flour, rice, beans, dehydrated soup, and ton after ton of other food items, including almonds, canned goods, pasta, sauerkraut, breakfast cereal, nutritional supplements and more! We loaded hospital beds, mattresses, surgical gloves, skin lotions, exam tables, dental chairs, false teeth, pain killers, T-shirts, sweat shirts and crate upon crate of brand new designer tennis shoes!

Since Sondra and I had multiple responsibilities, we were not able to depart with the rest of the crew as they began the voyage across the Atlantic aboard Spirit, but we knew we would be joining them off and on during the journey and for the stay in Russia. As we stood on the banks of the channel, watching the Spirit sail through Angels Gate again and out to sea, we glanced at our watches and laughed. The date was July 1; the time—five minutes to midnight!

We planned a brief stop at Corinto, Nicaragua, deciding then to head for the Soviet seaport of Riga, about 300 miles south of the city of Leningrad. A stronghold for the navy, Riga harbored a famous nuclear submarine base. We chose Riga rather than Leningrad because we heard the Leningrad-based mafia had plans to interfere with our cargo.

The supplies would be received in Riga and a portion trucked to Leningrad for a big evangelistic crusade, where each individual attending would receive a gift of food. Then afterwards, pastors could load up their vehicles with Bible materials, seeds, dried soup, flour and sauerkraut. The remainder of cargo would be distributed through warehouses in Riga.

The twelve-day trip to Nicaragua was smooth and uneventful. We discharged nutritional supplements, clothing and building materials. I flew to Corinto to make sure the mission there was running smoothly as we had no time to spare on our transatlantic sail if we were to meet our timetable.

We sailed with the ship through the Panama Canal. Authorities there had decided to waive many of the normal fees charged for passing through to the Caribbean Sea. We were taken into the canal almost immediately upon arrival and enjoyed a beautiful day and night-time transit through the amazing Panama Canal. We got off the ship as she left the canal and flew back to Los Angeles.

Within a day, we received a phone call from the Blessings for Obedience Ham Radio Network. Spirit had reported hitting a heavy storm only 100 miles outside of Panama. The ham operator made a phone patch back to the ship, enabling me to discuss the situation with Jamie and Captain Folden. We decided it would be best to change course.

The new course would take the ship close to the Cuban shoreline. The crew, in an act of faith, took five-gallon buckets, loaded them with Spanish Bibles and sent them adrift toward the Cuban shoreline. The waves were right, the wind was right, and the currents were right for the Bibles to wash onto the shore of Cuba!

In early August, Sondra and I planned to fly to the Nord-

Ostee Canal in Germany and board the Spirit there. Our friends Tom and Dorothy Miller and their young daughter, Rachel, decided to accompany us. The five of us would sail into Riga as part of Spirit's crew, avoiding the need for complicated and restricted Soviet visas.

We received a phone call—within minutes of our arrival at a German hotel—from a pastor in Southern California whom I had met once at our office in San Pedro. He had just been contacted by a man who told him that Fidel Castro had requested that 100,000 Bibles be brought into Cuba. The pastor wanted to know if the Spirit ship might be interested in delivering them. I said, "Absolutely yes!" What a "coincidence" that even before Spirit hit her next port of call after setting Bibles adrift to Cuba, we were asked to take a hundred thousand more into this isolated nation.

The next day, we met the ship at the east end of the Nord-Ostee Canal, where the crew spent a day ashore enjoying Germany. Everyone had a wonderful, unexpected but well-deserved break and, at midnight, we weighed anchor for the U.S.S.R.

18

FINAL DAYS OF THE SOVIET EMPIRE

So, like I told you in the beginning of this story, we found ourselves facing the consequences of being smack in the middle of a hard-line communist coup d'état. As we listened with disbelief to Boris, our legal contact in Riga, telling us that Mikhail Gorbachev had been kidnapped (or killed), I began to evaluate the situation. Unfortunately, information was very scarce.

The cities were sealed off, and television, radio and telephone communications were completely cut. The military began to more strictly enforce laws that made it illegal to speak against the government.

We took a drive into town and saw the Soviet military "securing" the Latvian parliament building by storming its third-story windows. Concrete barricades and military guards appeared throughout the streets.

I rolled the facts over in my mind, wondering what significant risk lay ahead for the crew or ship. Ham radio picked up a message from a "partner" organization, who warned us to run, to depart immediately. They said to take the ship and crew to a neutral, safe port. But I thought that if we left, we might never be able to get back in the country again with the new hard-line communists seizing control. The Lord had given us a job to do and we hadn't done it yet. It seemed clear that we needed to stay and complete our assignment.

I called the whole crew together to make an announcement. Realizing that we had women and children aboard , I expected at least some of them to be afraid. But, to my surprise, the entire crew was stronger than ever.

"What a great time to be alive!" some of them proclaimed. "Just think of it. Here in Russia at the hour of their greatest need!"

Others said with great conviction, "We didn't come all this way to run or hide. We're staying!" Many grabbed their backpacks, filled them full of gospel literature and Bibles, and went down the gangway into town to proclaim the name of the Lord. It was fun and easy. All you had to do was to speak English loud enough to be heard. As soon as the people knew you were Americans, crowds would gather and anxiously receive whatever you had to give. The ship's children actively participated in the ministry as our school students received a history lesson like none other! One crew family had six children ranging in age from seven to twenty. Eleven year-old Rachel, the daughter of our friends Tom and Dorothy, faithfully journeyed into town each day, and she alone distributed thousands and thousands of Russian gospel tracts to the people of Latvia.

In spite of all the commotion, we were able to complete the Customs paperwork. By the end of the day, we had clearance to unload without any taxes on the cargo or charges for any ship services, including moorage, wharfage, pilots, tugboats, water, longshoreman, or use of equipment. We were also free to give all the cargo to the churches, who in turn could distribute it without anything being diverted into government hands.

That night, the crew reported that tanks and armored personnel carriers were all over Riga. In town, a man was shot and killed by automatic weapons only a short distance from my grown son, Ron, who was with us as a bridge officer on Spirit.

The Soviet army and people were tense, quiet and frightened. Sometimes screaming and sirens could be heard throughout the area.

The next day, the Millers, Sondra and I were out strolling around and found ourselves at a dangerous "hot spot." We were in a city square, surrounded by tall brick buildings and beautiful old church steeples from long time past. We heard a sound from the sky and looked up to see prehistoric-looking Soviet helicopter-gunships, laden with rockets and Gatling guns, flying over us, around the church steeples and just barely above the roof tops. It was an awesome, yet sobering, sight.

People were yelling and chanting, women and children wailing and crying. Men were making gestures and shouting slogans at Russian soldiers. Standing on the steps in front of the doors of a main town square building, I put my camera up to my face, which was forbidden. I was wearing a bright orange neon T-shirt with Levis and white tennis shoes. This outfit being rare in the Soviet Union, at a distance I was easily recognizable as a U.S. citizen.

One particular helicopter pilot seemed to stall in the air and stare straight at me. Then he pointed the nose of the helicopter right into the camera lens and came swooping straight in my direction. *Wow*, I thought, as I continued to film him. "Whip, whip, whip" went the helicopter blades as he flew in at me, lifted over my head and banked away.

From the other side of the tall building came another prehistoric creature. The pilot came around, stalled in about the same place as the other pilot had, and took a hard look at me. He changed direction and flew straight in at me. *Wow*, I thought again. *There sure is a lot of interest in me.*

People were hollering at me, but I couldn't understand their Russian and was busy with my camera. They tried to tell me that the Soviet soldiers were marching toward the building from each side. I found out later that I was standing on the steps of Radio Free Latvia, the next target of the hard-liners, and the helicopters were flying cover for the soldiers on the ground. The only thing standing between them and the front door of the radio station was a dumb American tourist in a orange neon shirt taking pictures!

The Latvian people were very frightened, not knowing what lay ahead. They were anxious to receive any news about God. We handed out Russian language gospel tracts by the thousands.

No matter how many tracts we brought to town, it was never enough.

The people who could speak English would hear our American voices and run over to us, saying, "Do you know what is happening to us? Do you understand? Go back and tell the Americans. Tell them what is happening so they will help us!" It was heart wrenching to realize that they were hoping beyond hope that someone, somewhere, would care and come to free them from the horrible bondage descending on them.

No one had been able to get a line through to the states and, though we had tried many times, we were told that none were available. Finally, on Wednesday, we were able to send out a fax to our main office.

(That faxed letter, reproduced here, was widely circulated among our friends in the U.S.A. Both the gravity and opportunity of our situation in Russia came to life in this correspondence, bringing many people to pray for our safety and effectiveness while there.)

```
FACSIMILE TRANSMISSION/ AUGUST 21, 1990/ FROM THE
SPIRIT SHIP AT THE PORT OF RIGA, LATVIA, TO
HEADQUARTERS, SAN PEDRO, CALIFORNIA

TO: RAY GEORGE, PARK WEST CHILDREN'S FUND, INC.
    FAX #:  (213) 831-3968

FROM: DON AND SONDRA TIPTON
      RIGA, LATVIA U.S.S.R.

Dear Ray:

Crew is doing terrific. Sure love and miss you.
Sorry communications are so weak. It sometimes takes
days to get out a call.

We so much want to hear how things are going there.
Are there any problems with the port, is the crew
getting along, loving each other like they should,
are the trucks running, how is the food coming in,
how are you holding up under the stress of what has
```

been happening to us, etc. Please call Dr. McKeown and tell him everything is a go here - it's all right on time. Look forward to seeing his smiling face.

It was very tense here for awhile, but God gave us the courage to stick it out. We were advised to leave immediately, to run for a neutral port, but if we had left, we may not have been able to come back and leave food here for our brothers and sisters and their children. They would have been facing a severe winter with little food under the new hard line communist dictatorship. We had already received permission to unload and the declarations were signed for the churches to receive the food.

To see the Soviet tanks in the streets, helicopter gunships flying low overhead, laden with rockets and Gatling guns, the army storming buildings, firing machine guns over the heads of running crowds. A man was shot and killed a short distance from my son. People were crying, shouting. But we still felt it was a chance we had to take. It was a hard decision to make, maybe the hardest ever. The sense of responsibility was so great for the men, the women and the children aboard. But this is what we came for. We knew from the first day we started this ministry that these kinds of decisions may fall upon us. We were so proud to see our crew, in the midst of all this craziness, all over town passing out tracts and proclaiming the good news. The idea of running never seemed to enter their minds. If we would have run, we would have lost the great opportunity to witness the gospel and see the mighty hand of the Lord and miracles sweeping right before our face.

Sounds crazy to say but, I don't think the crew has ever had so much fun. Wish you were here, Ray. The old city and the architecture and the people make me know how much you would love it if you were here. The history goes back centuries.

We love you. Be of great courage! We know you're doing a superb job that allows us to stay here. Ray, feed the people and pray for them. Love them into the kingdom. Ask everyone in the food operation for a special prayer for us.

Love, Don and Sondra

Within a few days, the Latvians decided they'd had enough and declared independence. In Riga, the feared Oman or Black Berets special Soviet forces were in the process of storming the Latvian Parliament building, when it was rumored that the leader of the coup had shot himself. The others had been arrested or had fled, and Yeltsin was in temporary control of the country. The next thing we heard was that Gorbachev would soon be restored to power! No one really knew if this news was true. The rest of the world was receiving much more accurate reports on the situation than were we, right there in the middle of it!

On the evening of the fifth day, we were at the telephone company, trying to get a call out to the States when we saw people running through the streets. I thought for sure the tanks were back until two of our crew men ran in to tell us that the statue of Lenin was being taken down.

We rushed to the statue and joined hundreds of others who were watching as a crane hooked onto it and tried to rip it from its base. The crowd stared. An eerie silence was in the air, almost as if the people's god was being taken off his pedestal. For at least five decades, this man was like their Jesus, their Abe Lincoln, the George Washington of the Soviet Union. They had been taught in school from childhood to love, to fear and revere this man.

Now, here he was, with a giant crane and cable around his body, being ripped violently from his stand. I had told the crew members earlier that they were not to get involved in making any political statements. But this was a great day for the people, greater than they could imagine. It was the lifting of a great oppressor. *This can't pass in silence,* I thought.

Suddenly, an American voice rang out from the crowd, "Hang that turkey! Put the cable around his neck! Viva freedom! Down with oppression! Up with the people!" The people began to clap, cheer and shout. The still atmosphere was shattered.

The crazy American voice I heard was my own! There I was at the head of the crowd, embroiled in Soviet politics,

Images of the Soviet coup d'état

shouting loudly, starting a political riot. "Hang that turkey! Down with Lenin!"

With us that day was Ron Robertson, a wonderful Scotsman of Jewish descent, a missionary with a brave heart. He began to shout, even louder than the rest.

The army tried to hold us back and quiet us down. Ron was thinner than I and easier to push around. Every few minutes, the Soviet soldiers would pick him up and toss him into the crowd. I was amazed at how well he flew as he sailed past me. The crowd would catch him, stand him back to his feet and without hesitation, he'd run right back to the head of the crowd. What a time to be in the Soviet Union!

Later, I was presented with a large marble stone from the base of the statue—a prized possession.

After this momentous night, we completed off-loading the cargo, sent twenty big truckloads of food to Leningrad 300 miles away, and made plans to transport the crew. We had rented the giant 20,000 seat Olympic Sports Complex— which looked like the beautiful Forum in Los Angeles—for a great three day crusade. The price for renting the Sports Complex was a $150 a day (U.S. money), including lights, sound, and the entire use of the stadium. We couldn't believe the U.S. dollar to Soviet ruble rate of exchange.

The crew worked long but joyous hours packing up and handing out food, seeds and Christian books to the people who attended the crusade.

There is no way to describe the tremendous feeling of being with thousands of people who are hearing about Jesus for the first time in their lives and are rushing forward to embrace Him. There were seven meetings and, at each, we saw thousands of people come forward to receive the Lord. The Word was confirmed with miraculous healings. A blind man could see, a crippled lady could walk!

To our delight, word of this crusade reached Siberia, Chernobyl and the Ukraine. Underground pastors rode on trains

Days of great uncertainty. Statue of Lenin is yanked from its base.

for days or drove old trucks across country to attend. They brought their families and joyously gave thanks to God for their new-found freedom of religion and democracy. Finally, they were free to worship!

We had food and seed left over after these meetings and offered the goods to church pastors to take home. The men from Chernobyl didn't know which items to take first. Their ground had been horribly contaminated by the great nuclear disaster five years before, so they were thrilled beyond words to have food and seed that was clean and pure.

When we returned to Riga, the crew began to visit the square of the Latvian freedom statue on a nightly basis, singing, dancing and preaching. And every night, many, many people received Jesus.

Some six weeks after entering Soviet waters, the great ship Spirit pointed her bow toward home. She sailed out of the Baltic Sea, burning 2,000 gallons of fuel each day (that's $1,600 per day), not counting the oil and lubricants, and the wear and tear on all the ship's moving parts.

She sailed past Sweden, Germany, Denmark, and through the English channel, beginning her crossing of the Atlantic Ocean. Making a hard right around Cuba into the Gulf of Mexico, she made her final approach to Galveston, Texas. Her brave crew was tired but ready to go again, excitedly anticipating the cargo they would be loading.

Still, after all these miracles, more miracles were required to keep the operations going. Just because we had trusted God in the past did not automatically make us trust for the future. Each time is new and each time is hard. We struggle like all other Christians.

Sondra and I flew home four weeks before the ship returned. In our office at the Los Angeles harbor, I paced the floor, concerned about the lack of provisions for the returning ship. I started a conversation with the Lord that went like this: "Lord, your Spirit ship is now two weeks from arriving in Galveston;

"Spirit" children passing out Gospel tracts (top) Soldiers hungry for the Gospel (middle-left) the Olympic Stadium in Leningrad (middle-right) where thousands of people received Jesus as their Lord and Savior (lower)

that's 1,700 miles from here. She's arriving empty of any food to feed the crew. I don't know how many of the crew will leave her and how many will stay. We need 250,000 gallons of fuel upon arrival and it is now most expensive!

"We don't even have enough fuel in the gas tank of our Peterbilt truck for it to make a run to Galveston. I've never been to Galveston. I don't know anyone in Galveston or anywhere else in the entire Gulf of Mexico.

"In two weeks, it will be me, Lord, that everyone will be looking to, saying, 'Where is everything? We're hungry. The ship generators will quit if there's no fuel for the engines. The ship will go dark and cold. And there's no cargo to put in the ship.

"Lord, that's ten million pounds of cargo we need. And we're broke again; we don't have a dime. Lord, I just want to go on record: **You're** the provider. We have really got to see big miracles now. But if you're not in this, God now, I want out now. I put my trust in you."

As I walked the floor, for me, this really was a supreme test. Everything was absolutely out of my hands. I had no control over anything whatsoever. I felt helpless and small. Almost no cargo had come in the whole time we were in Russia. It was very sparse. And even if I had ten million pounds of goods, just how would I transport it all the way to the Gulf?

Now, once again, we would see the mighty hand of God. Who could deny that only God could help us, as He had done so many times for us in the past?

Then, as in the past, the miracle floodgates burst open. Kellogg's called to say they had thirteen boxcars of cereal that had just been made, but with the wrong date stamped on the box. They couldn't open the boxes and repack them, and they couldn't sell them. They would have to pay to have it hauled to the dump and buried. If we would take it out of their market area, they would give it to us.

Southern Pacific Railway said, "If they'll give the product, we'll transport it for free." By the time the ship arrived in

Galveston, train cars were waiting. Eleven truckloads of a complete hospital were donated, ready to erect. Boxcar loads of "Top Ramen" dehydrated noodles and Nissin "Cup a Soup" were sent again by free rail.

We asked the railroad for even more boxcars to transport Bible literature and tracts. Thousands and thousands of pounds of seed came out of the Midwest. Truck after truck began arriving in the Port of Galveston. The rail cars were stacked down the tracks. Trucks filled with sacks of flour were backing down the docks, as well as truckloads of wheat and sugar. We received baby food, canned fish and cooking oil, thousands upon thousands of pounds of clothes and, literally, truckloads of multivitamins.

Within a couple of weeks, all the fuel the ship could hold was donated plus some 10,000 gallons of oil. A satellite communication phone was donated to the ship, and the great Port of Galveston—as well as Customs—waived every single charge and fee. The longshoremen's union waived all their fees as well. So did the tugboat companies. The Lord caused everyone to help.

As we prayed for a destination, the Lord put on our hearts the distant drums of Africa. Spirit's belly began to swell and fill with every good thing God would send to these faraway nations. Some crew members were faint and weary from the battle and left for home. But most stood brave and fast. (How we thank God for our crew and appreciate their faithfulness!)

I was working on several projects in Los Angeles and was so busy I never even saw the great ship Spirit in Galveston. But when the ship pulled out, she looked like one of those Haitian freighters, the decks stacked high with every imaginable thing!

It was so crystal clear. Success in serving God wasn't based on me, or on anyone's great knowledge of the Bible or thundering spiritual ability, but on the love that God has for the poor, hungry and dying people who are perishing without knowing His great love!

We were just Christ's hands extended. We were willing— not able. Only in Him are all things possible.

19

GO UGLY EARLY

The Spirit's next voyage was to Angola, Africa, and although the mission was a tremendous success, the return voyage proved to be a supreme test of our faith. Ship's Chaplain Doug Ford and ship's Steward Vinicio Alvarez both contracted cerebral malaria by way of mosquitoes in Luanda, Angola. Both men died. Doug, who had loved and ministered to all he met, left behind a wife and two children. Our beloved Vinicio, a young Guatemalan man only 21 years old, had touched us all with his joyful worship of the Lord.

We had trusted God all along for everything. We trusted him for ships, for our food, clothes and shelter, for millions of dollars worth of cargo and hundreds of thousands of gallons of fuel. We had trusted him for safety at sea, for the protection of our crew during perilous ship repairs and dangerous cargo operations, and we had trusted him for favor with the Coast Guard, Customs, Immigration and favor with foreign governments.

Could we continue to trust Him now that we had been asked to sacrifice two of our much-loved soldiers? Could we continue to rely on Him when circumstances made no sense? When a young man, barely more than a boy, and a cherished husband and father of two, were suddenly snatched from our midst, could we still trust God?

We had asked for their healing, having fasted and prayed. We had cried and screamed out to God to call breath back into their lifeless bodies.

Doug was buried at sea on Easter Sunday, and Vinnie's body

was flown from a tropical disease center in Fortaleza, Brazil, to Guatemala for burial. We'd lost them; we had to accept that and go on. Although we all knew these men had come to the ship led by God, the thought plagued me that I was somehow responsible for their death by encouraging them to serve God on the ship. In my presentation of the wonderful life we lead, I had personally told them how He provides for our needs and protects us. How could their families forgive me, I agonized? What a heart wrenching period this was for us all.

Carla Ford, Doug's widow, displayed great strength in the days that followed Doug's death. A few days after the funeral, Carla made an announcement to the crew. She reminded us that her whole family had been called to the Spirit by God, not Doug alone. She firmly stated that even though Doug was gone, the Ford family intended to stay on the ship, the home that God had given them.

Ironically, this tragic incident seemed to strengthen the crew, rather than weaken them, as we all came to realize the gravity of the mission to which we were called. Almost the entire crew decided to stay with the ship, and even more than in the past, they exuded a fearlessness, a battle-hardened steel in their back bones. They had endured tremendous hardship and the Lord had brought them through. But now, without doubt, all of us knew that **even our very lives** may be required!

In the first four and a half years of operation, Friend Ships delivered cargo to more than thirty foreign nations, including Albania, Croatia, Sierra Leone, Liberia, Ghana, Gambia, Nicaragua, El Salvador, Guatemala, Haiti, Honduras and the U.S.S.R. Spirit weathered storms, hurricanes, invasions, embargoes, wars and even the Soviet coup d'état.

❖❖❖

What do you think, friends? Is this the tale of a group of good-hearted people who wanted to make a difference in the world, did a lot of positive thinking and hit on a workable idea?

Is this simply a giant success story, a nonstop series of fortunate coincidences?

Or is this the account of a great God, a God who loves people, loves the poor and wants his children to serve Him?

We are here to tell you that " Friend Ships" is a testimony to the God of Provision, the Maker of Heaven and Earth, who owns the world and everyone in it. Positiveness, coincidence or good ideas simply had no part in the story you've just read. If you look closely with an open mind, our experiences reveal the true heart of our Lord and Savior.

The Word of God tells us to *"defend the cause of the weak and fatherless; maintain the rights of the poor and the oppressed and rescue the weak and needy."* It says to *"Command those who are rich in this present world not to be arrogant nor to put their hope in wealth, which is so uncertain, but to put their hope in God, who richly provides us with everything for our enjoyment. Command them to do good, to be rich in deeds, and to be generous and willing to share."*

You may say, "I'm not rich." But, please recognize, even if all you did was eat your fill yesterday, you're far ahead of a billion and a half people in the world! And according to the measuring stick of the impoverished, even you are among the extremely wealthy of this world.

We read the Bible and even memorize a few scriptures, like John 3:16 and Romans 10:10. We base our hope and all of eternity on these verses, but if they are true, **so are all the others in the Bible**. Let's not confine our belief in God's Word to only a few scriptures.

The miracle of salvation is the greatest experience of a Christian's life, but that's only the beginning. What about the rest of God's Word? What of the many passages about the *"royal law"* to *"love your neighbor as yourselves"?* What about the hundreds of instructions to help the poor? How about the good Samaritan and Jesus' examples of feeding thousands?

In Acts 6, the disciples realized that part of their responsibility while preaching the gospel must be to look after widows in distress. To lead this important work of God they chose from among them a man full of wisdom and God's grace and power, a great warrior in Christ—Stephen—the gospel's first recorded martyr!

The Bible says that, *"Whoever is kind to the needy honors God."* Isaiah tells us that the kind of fast God has chosen is *"to loose the chains of injustice and untie the cords of the yoke, to set the oppressed free and break every yoke. Is it not to share your food with the hungry and to provide the poor wanderer with shelter"*... *"when you see the naked to clothe him."*

Jesus says that when we give food to one who is hungry, give drink to one who is thirsty, provide shelter to a stranger, offer clothes to someone in need or visit a prisoner or one who is sick, it is as if we do this very thing for the Lord Himself!

In the Bible, James asks the question, *"Suppose a brother or sister is without clothes and daily food. If one of you says to him, 'Go, I wish you well; keep warm and well fed, but does nothing about his physical needs, what good is it? In the same way, faith by itself, if it is not accompanied by action, is dead. But someone will say, 'You have faith; I have deeds.' Show me your faith without deeds, and I will show you my faith by what I do."*

John asks, *"If anyone has material possessions and sees his brother in need but has no pity on him, how can the love of God be in him? Let us not love with words or tongue but with actions and in truth."*

James also teaches that the *"Religion that God our Father accepts as pure and faultless is this: to look after orphans and widows in their distress and to keep oneself from being polluted by the world."*

How can anyone listen to these scriptures and not think God wants us to do all we can to help the poor?

Many people believe that if we stand on faith, our prayers will be answered, but the Bible tells us that love is greater than faith. What if we stand on faith and add to it love—love for our brother, love for our neighbor, love for our enemy, love for a stranger? God tells us that *"Love never fails"* and *"Faith without deeds is dead."* Deeds are love. Mix love and faith into one container—your faith with God's love—and you have an explosive ingredient beyond what any container can hold. It's beyond ballistic, beyond nuclear. You are that container. Indeed you are His hand extended.

In the book of Exodus, the Lord describes those who volunteered to help build His tabernacle. *"And everyone who was **willing** and whose heart moved him came...All who were **willing**, men and women alike...He has filled them with skill to do all kinds of work."*

It's through you, His children, that God will work His miracles. It's through you that God will reach the child. But, God is the ultimate gentleman. He wants to move **with** you in love—in an agreement of love. Your agreement is required, your participation is required, **your willingness is required**.

James says that *"judgment without mercy will be shown to anyone who has not been merciful,"* and that *"Mercy triumphs over judgment."* How many of us are praying for ourselves or a loved one who is sick but have no mercy toward the 35,000 children a day who are dying? The Bible says, *"If a man shuts his ears to the cry of the poor, he too will cry out and not be answered."* It also says that *"He who gives to the poor will lack nothing, but he who closes his eyes to them receives many curses."*

Matthew tells us that those who turned away from one in need, turned away from the Lord and were sent to eternal punishment, for *"I was hungry and you gave me nothing to eat."*

In the Bible we read that *"A generous man will himself be blessed, for he shares his food with the poor,"* and that *"He who is kind to the poor lends to the Lord, and He will reward him for what he has done."* Jesus says, *"Give, and it will be given to you. A good measure, pressed down, shaken together and running over...for with the measure you use, it will be measured to you."*

Paul tells us that "*Each man should give what he has decided in his heart to give...God loves a cheerful giver...*" and that "*he who supplies seed to the sower and bread for food will also supply and increase your store of seed and will enlarge the harvest of your righteousness. You will be made rich in every way*" [But why? And this is a key] "*so that you can be generous on every occasion*" and continue to give out to others that which God has given to you!

God wants us to invest our time and resources wisely. The book of Matthew tells us that a servant who multiplied five talents given to him is commended by his master. The servant who is afraid to take a chance on losing what he has been given and does not multiply it but hides it in the ground, greatly displeases his master.

Jesus tells us a story about a farmer who went out to sow his seed. Some seed dropped onto the path and birds came and ate it up. Some fell on rocky places where there wasn't much soil. It sprang up, but died quickly because it had no roots. Some seed fell among thorns, and the thorns choked the plant. But some seed fell on good soil and produced thirty, sixty or one hundred times what was sown. Jesus tells us that the seed is the Word of God and because of lack of understanding, trouble, persecution, the worries of life, or deceitfulness of wealth, the seed does not produce fruit. The seed that does produce a good yield does so because the person hearing the Word, understands it and acts upon it.

It is hard to speak to someone about the gospel when they are hungry. It's hard for them to understand it. But come to them with love in the form of physical assistance and they **experience, firsthand,** the love of Christ. Some think the commodities that we load aboard our ships are only "food", "medicine" or "clothes." But those commodities are "love." We deliver love in action. We bring the Word in action. We plow the ground and till the soil with love. We prepare it for the seed of the gospel.

❖❖❖

❖❖❖

"How do I know what God has called me to do?" This is the question I am asked more than any other. If your heart yearns to serve God but you don't know how to do it, find a man or woman who is already doing something that is laid out in the Bible and help them. If a man in your church preaches on the city street corner, don't criticize him because you can't (or won't) do what he is doing. Help him. Hold a flashlight on his Bible while he reads, intercede for him in prayer, wash his car so that he has more time to preach. Push him toward the mark.

If you were a father with an estate and had given your eldest son the job of mowing the lawn, wouldn't it thrill you to look out the window and see your younger son, who had not yet received his own assignment, pushing against his brother's back, helping to move the lawn mower, anxious to further the needs of his Father's house?

Help your brother, and before long the Lord will clarify your mission. Be tenacious. God is with you—who can be against you?

Satan is a liar. He's all smoke and mirrors. He makes you believe that he has the ultimate power and strength, but Jesus defeated Satan at the cross. We are the ones Jesus died for. You have the weapons and the power. Take control. You know Satan is our adversary, so don't wait for him to knock you down before you go on the offensive against him. Be aggressive. Get tough. Get in Satan's face and "go ugly early."

We are men and women of purpose. Your birth was no mistake, and it's no coincidence that you've been chosen to live in a time such as this. There is a reason you're on this earth. Your life is constantly full of great opportunity. God awaits your decisions—the choices are yours.

You are children of the living God, saved by grace, *"not by works, so that no one can boast."* But remember, that the same passage continues on to say that we are *"created in Christ Jesus* **to do good works, which God prepared in advance for us to** *do.*" It would be foolish for us to think that God has given us work to do, put it in our hearts and then made no provisions for it. How can we think this of our Father who is the God of Provision?

Some feel that when we give money to the church or to the mission field, we are financing God. Let's get this straight. God does not need our financing. He doesn't wake up every morning and check the stock market or the value of the dollar against the yen. No, God blesses us with an opportunity to be part of His work by allowing us the chance to give money or to give of ourselves. Money is precious to most people, so the issue often centers on cash. How easily we forget that God is the one who *"gives you the ability to produce wealth."* God is God. He gives us everything we have, even every breath we take.

But if we are wise enough to partake of the opportunity He offers, we will give our finances—and we will give the one thing far more precious to Him than money.

Imagine Jesus approaching you with a collection basket in His hand. If the Great Giver Himself stood before you with His eyes of love and His nail-scarred hands, what kind of an offering might He receive? How excited you would be to give! You'd probably pull out every last dollar you had as He stood there in front of you with His old woven basket.

But I know well, and can say with assurance that what He really would want to know as He gazed into your eyes is, **"How much of yourself are you willing to place into my basket?"**

We know how much of Himself He poured out for you. He valued you above all else. You are the jewels, the fine gold, the rubies, in His sight.

Remember, you are the one He loves, and in this day and even this hour, you can choose what to give to God. Take courage. Believe what He has put in your heart. Spread the gospel, feed the hungry, love your neighbor, visit the sick. You're not waiting for God. He's waiting for you. Let today be your day of decision.

Move by the Word of God. Don't be faint. Act on what God

puts in your heart. Stand and believe Him. Take hold of it and don't let go.

Maybe you have a dream hidden in your heart, something you have longed to do for your Lord Jesus ever since you were born again. Why aren't you doing it? If it builds the Father's house, Jesus will give you all you need. Be bold, be brave. Trust God. Don't let fear be your companion. *"From the days of John the Baptist until now, the kingdom of heaven has been forcefully advancing and forceful men lay hold of it!"* Let it be the last thing you're willing to give up.

Time after time God reaches down in love and assures us in His Word, saying *"Fear not!"* Advance and seek the kingdom and everything you need will be supplied to you. He promises, *"Do not be afraid, little flock, for your Father has been pleased to give you the kingdom."*

Become committed personally, prayerfully and financially in spreading the gospel and in helping those in need. Step forward. Be involved in whatever way you possibility can. It's God's will. He is the Lord. It's important to Him. He will appreciate it, it honors Him, He will bless you for it, He will multiply your efforts.

Work with great tenacity! It doesn't matter how knowledgeable, attractive, well dressed, well spoken, affluent or even how wise you are. If you do not sink your teeth in and hang on like a bulldog, you will fail.

The world wants you to fail. The enemy wants you to fail. At times, even some Christians want you to fail, but God wants you to win. If you stick with Him, only Him, and are not willing to be led by circumstances, even when it's the death of your friends, He can and He will, bring you through. The journey may not be easy and not without disappointments, heartaches and scars. Maybe even your life will be required, but the commitment will be worth it because this is what you were created to do.

If you are willing to work for His glory and His alone, then ask Jesus to make the way. Cast down the fears that stand in your way. Don't look at the circumstances. Don't look to the left or the right. Keep your eyes only on Him.

❖❖❖

The task set before you may be impossible to accomplish in your eyes but, with Jesus, all things are possible. It probably won't be easy, friends, but the Lord will make it happen. As He's filled our lives with joy unspeakable, He will fill yours!

We praise and give honor to our wonderful Lord and King!

"Friend Ship Hope carries disaster relief equipment (including helicopter), relief workers and medical teams to people in times of need".

Largest cargo airplane in the world, a Russian Antonov 124 full of food to Moscow
Russian soldiers help discharge the cargo (upper left)

Scriptures Used in Chapter 19

For your own personal study and blessing, we recommend looking up each scripture used in chapter nineteen. Use your chosen version of the Bible to check our application of the verses and their use in context. May God speak to you as you study.

1. Psalm 82:3-4
2. I Timothy 6:17-18
3. James 2:8
4. Proverbs 14:31
5. Isaiah 58:6-7
6. James 2:15-18
7. I John 3:17-18
8. James 1:27
9. I Corinthians 13:8
10. James 2:26
11. Exodus 35:21,22,37
12. James 2:13
13. Proverbs 21:13
14. Proverbs 28:27
15. Matthew 25:42
16. Proverbs 22:9
17. Proverbs 19:17
18. Luke 6:38
19. II Corinthians 9:7-11
20. Matthew 25
21. Matthew 13
22. Ephesians 2:8-10
23. Deuteronomy 8:18
24. Matthew 11:12
25. Luke 12:32

EPILOGUE

Jesus & Company (Part I) doesn't even begin to record all the miracles our mighty God has performed since the inception of Friend Ships. In the less-than-ten years of Friend Ships' existence, so many lives have been touched by God that ten volumes could not include every exciting story. We have recounted but a few of the many thousands which demonstrate the love of Jesus for His children.

We hope to put more in writing, so you can enjoy heartwarming stories about the ever-expanding food program (which, at the writing of this book, distributes enough food locally for **150,000 meals per week**)—so you can thrill along with us as you see miracles surrounding the new ship "Faithful" (soon to set sail for Jesus)—so you can experience the tremendous crusades in Africa (and the hilarious escapades in Albania)—but most of all so you can be encouraged to also step out and walk in faith where you've never dreamed of walking before.

This book and those to follow are all records of the faithfulness of our ever-present, ever-loving, ever-giving Lord and Savior, Jesus Christ.

There is no end to this book because there is no end to the work God has for all of us to do. So until He comes, we serve—and want you to serve—with joy.

PRAYER TO GOD

As you saw from the pages of this book, God, the Creator and Giver of Life does care about each of us. We want to say that you too can know Him and His wonderful plan for your life. But, God is Holy and must be approached on His terms. He wants you to worship Him as the only God in your life. Just as the first people, Adam and Eve failed to trust God, so all of us have sinned by trying to run our own lives without God.

The Bible says that even if you obey all of God's laws but one, you are a lawbreaker and a guilty sinner before Him. So, no matter how religious you might be, or how many good deeds you may have done, you can never measure up to God's holiness. You are lost and separated from God.

But God understands your helplessness and He loves you so much that He arranged to have His Son take your punishment and die for your sins. The Bible says, *"The wages of sin is death, but the gift of God is eternal life through Jesus Christ our Lord."* Salvation is a gift. It can't be worked for, so no one can boast about earning it.

In the Bible, John chapter 3, Jesus told a religious leader, Nicodemus, that he must be born again to have eternal life; so you too must be born spiritually into God's family. That is why you need to invite Jesus to come into your life and to forgive you of your sin.

If you want to become a child of God and have Jesus as your Savior, speak right now to God. You can pray these words:
Dear God,
I recognize my sin and rebellion against you. Thank you for allowing Jesus to take the punishment for my sin by dying on the cross. I would like Jesus to come into my life, to be my Savior, and my Lord. Thank you Jesus for coming into my life. Amen

If you just prayed that prayer, and you want to know more about God, there are three things you should do:
You need to talk to God often in prayer,
you need to listen to Him by reading His words, the Bible and you need to find a church where people love God and His Word, so you can get to know Him better.

If you'd like to receive more information on how to begin your new walk with the Lord, please write to the address on the next page, and we will send you a free booklet.

For additional copies of
Jesus & Company (Part1) or
for more information, contact:

Friend Ships Unlimited
1019 N. 1st Avenue
Lake Charles, LA
www.friendships.org
Phone: (337) 433-5022